WITHIN IS THE FOUNTAIN

AUTHOR—GOD
SAGE—LEONORA NICHOLS
NEW ORLEANS, USA

Two Dragons International Inc.

New Orleans, Louisiana & Potomac Falls, Virginia

First Edition 2007

ISBN: 978-0-9816467-2-5

Printed in the United States of America.

Introduction

by Sir George Trevelyan

There is a real place for books which have the authentic ring of the Christ Source speaking within. For many people they are invaluable for reading in bed before we put out the light and turn to sleep, for the entry into sleep in lifted mood is of paramount importance. I think of volumes I have loved and treasured: "God Calling" and Christ in You", by Two Listeners (anonymous), "God Spoke to Me" by Eileen Caddy, "The Quiet Mind" by Grace Cooke. Here is another of great beauty, coming clearly from the same high source. The title expresses the great truth: "Within is the Fountain".

I recommend it to you not only as an excellent bedside book, but because it points the way for which we all must strive. A spiritual awakening is taking place on a wide front. It manifests in an infinite diversity of expression, as if a flood of new consciousness and spiritual energy is beginning to flow. Many have gone questing for gurus and much study is given to the spiritual teachers. But in the last years many have learned that ultimately the only real teacher is within us.

As Browning wrote:

"Truth is within ourselves. It takes no rise
From outward things whate'er you may believe.
There is an inner centre in us all
Where Truth abides in fullness, but around
Wall upon wall the gross flesh hems it in
That perfect clear perception which is Truth."

We live in dramatic days when change is foreseen on all levels. Everything points to the likelihood of a great transformation of consciousness in Western man before the end of the century. This may be accompanied by outward changes, which must be accepted and welcomed as a cleansing of the polluted planet, but for each one of us the challenge and responsibility is to take control of ourselves--the one part of the universe we really possess and can change.

Thus in these years there is nothing more important than finding the Inner Teacher. Truly this is the way to God, for the I AM is the Voice of God. All outward study and questing leads to the same goal--the Divine within each of us. Here is the ending of the Grail Quest, so relevant to our time.

This little book is a beautiful example of the goal achieved. It has the authentic ring of the Divine Voice speaking within. Not only is it inspiring reading, full of wisdom, but it encourages us to feel that we too may achieve this power of inner listening, so that in time the Voice may begin to speak to us and direct our lives. The authoress, Leonora Nichols, lives in Virginia. She is a beloved friend of many concerned with the present quickening of the spirit. Yet this writing is beyond personality and the name is therefore hardly relevant. The Journal, received and written down over two years, is full of treasures of wisdom and joy. The Christ speaks in this way within us and our lives our changed.

May this Journal encourage many to work towards their own conscious contact with the Source within. There is a shift now from the earlier trance mediumship to an inner clair-audience, a listening to the voice. We need not greatly fear deceiving ourselves. Even if at first we are really talking to ourselves and writing down the results, it can be valuable as an exercise. But it is a common experience that when the Voice within really speaks, there is no doubt of its reality. More and more people will find the Christ flow within in the coming years.

We are all on a spiritual journey, and Leonora's contribution by publishing her inspired writings will certainly be an encouragement to many to work for their own contact.

I most heartily recommend, "Within is the Fountain" to all who are involved in the movement for spiritual awakening, which may ultimately be the salvation of mankind.

Sir George Trevelyan (1906–1996) was an educational pioneer, a founding father of the New Age movement, furniture maker and visionary. Noted author his books include: "A Vision of the Aquarian Age" (1977), "Operation Redemption" (1981), "Summons to a High Crusade" (1985).

To Leonora

I Kept My Promise

Within Is The Fountain

The Beginning—Date Unknown

Be still, my child, and write. For the time has come for me to speak. But I speak only when man gives fully and absolutely his Being to Me, where I AM. Now be very still and write only what you are hearing inwardly that the Truth which you seek in your deep heart may be further revealed and more fully experienced.

The human mind with its personality must be very carefully and purposefully disciplined and prepared that the full glory of the indwelling Christ may shine out. This is the purpose of this effort. This is what you long for and this promise is within your reach, for it is written within your Being. But there must be a more consecrated effort, or discipline. The Promise is there, already to shine out in all its glory and effulgence. You have but to keep this goal ever before your inward vision, and hold your attention upon It.

This is the sacred privilege, or gift of God the Father, to man. He ever awaits, deep within the Heart.

This is the Eternal Truth which all must seek and understand in order to grow into the Immortal Being made in His Image.

How else can you receive Him unless you seek Him where He is and set your heart upon Him where He awaits you.

If your dearest friend on earth awaits you in your home, your house, and you are forever wandering abroad, how can you meet him and glory in his friendship and companionship?

So it is with the indwelling Christ.
Think deeply on this.

Date Unknown

As you deepen your stillness, your Communion with me, the more creative you will become.

This is the great paradox. To be deeply quiet, consciously quiet, brings you into the Universal Womb of Creation, into the peace that is productive. To let your mind be repeatedly brought back to worldthought, with its disquieting images, robs you of the peace that is needed for spiritual progress and understanding.

It would be wise, therefore, during the days activities, to watch your thoughts, and to remind yourself, frequently, of this profound Truth, that your spiritual destiny unfolds from the deep inner calm and serenity of the soul, and never in the flux of the phenomenal world.

Date Unknown

The advantage of writing as you are doing is that it makes possible the necessary discipline. There is less interference, both mental and physical, as you write in this fashion. The concentration that is needed has been achieved, enabling you to listen and hear the Voice within: Thus, communication becomes possible.

Everything rests upon this listening and stillness. Deep meditation is another matter, and a withdrawn, cloistered life is not a necessity at this time, for the objective is to gather together those souls who are capable of Communion (in one form or another) that we may be able to use those who shall be the Forerunners or nucleus of the New Humanity.

Always remember that this moment on earth is the apogee of an age, an age that has peaked to its limit in defiance of the Law, and therefore, must destroy itself, that the waters of Life may rise again, purified, as a New Wave, a New Earth, a New Race.

Understand this, for the disappearance of the old will inevitably take place.

It is of great importance therefore that this is understood, lest the souls we have need of be overcome with panic and thereby be lost in the breaking up of the old.

Date Unknown

In times of stress to be in command requires the discipline we have been emphasizing throughout these communications. If you constantly finger with thy mind the condition you wish to be free of, the law of truth cannot operate for *no* admixture is possible here. Truth is absolute. To dwell in the Soul is to wall off, as out of bounds, the stuff of the lower form from thy activating mind with its fears.

The form is but a fleeting phenomena. It has no substance other than that.

When you identify the consciousness with the bodily defect that you wish to be rid of, you are entangling its image with the power of your mind, and thereby strengthening its hold, its reflection on consciousness, and so on the body.

To be free of all that is alien to Truth, the mind must be held steady and steadfast in the Center or Citadel of thy soul.

Understand this.

November 3, 1975

Have confidence—relax your hold on consciousness, and write only that which flows through your mind, from moment to moment—unobstructed by the personal will or thoughts. This is what you have been praying for and it will clarify itself as you go along.

The earth, the planet, is receiving new energies in preparation for the New Dispensation. It is necessary, therefore, for all those who are open to the New to drop all preconceived thoughts or ideas. These radiant energies, which are flowing from vast centres of cosmic light, are making these communions possible.

Do not, therefore, intrude your thought upon this effort—lest you inject old thought forms, into it, but be deeply still and write only that which is flowing into your mind spontaneously—and remember all that forms within your thought patterns in this fashion comes from the interior world of spirit—of Light.

This is the work laid out for you at the present time. The important thing for you to remember is the Now. The living present moment. Take hold of the Now. It is ripe with Truth and Light. Again, I say, let it flow.

Light is the key to the New Age. The forces of darkness, which are dominating the planet at this time can flourish and function only in darkness.

Children of Light, rejoice, for God is not mocked, and He is here. So fear not.

November 4, 1975

Be still deeply still, and then open wide your mind and heart in expectancy of the Divine, who ever seeks channels through which to speak to men. Your purpose now is to be one of those channels. This means dedicated period of quiet that these communions can continue.

We see into the hearts of men, thereby we find our own.

You are not, again we must emphasize this, you are not the personal self, which you appear to be. Your tendency is to judge according to the form, the appearance.

This is the work we have laid out for you, to constantly center your consciousness, your attention, on the invisible One, thereby releasing its Light and Truth. There is no other way to the spiritual "breakthrough" which you are seeking.

Above all, there must be no false pride or vanity in this work. All me and mine must be displaced by Thine.

Clear the mind of all doubt and criticism. These are deadly foes that must go.

These preliminary notes are only a preface to the work which will follow.

Today we will tell you about our aim. For the present it is simply to train you in obedience that you may be of use. Listen carefully, in stillness, and clear the mind of all past, accumulated beliefs, that the Word may become flesh, or manifest.

"Being is the Word made Flesh." You prayed for the Truth of being, and God spoke those words directly to you. Being is the I AM. Your individualized being, or I

AM, is God spoken forth (the Word) and made Flesh or manifest in the physical world. This is the Truth of all mankind. Being is Seed Word in all created life, and like all seeds it must be nurtured and cherished and given the beneficent conditions for growth and flowering.

This is our first lesson for you. Concentrate, as much as possible, on the Being aspect of yourself. It holds the eternal reflection or Image of the One.

By so doing, all the dross and nonsense of the world-self will fall away into its native nothingness.

Remember it is the Divine you are seeking. And what He reveals is Himself—so there can be no grasping here. The Light is impersonal, this you must understand. It is not yours, so to speak, but God's, and the slightest egoistic attitude will blunt the thrust of its power. It is always the question of breaking up the old egoistic patterns that the Universal may find its expression.

The ego, small and pitiful as it generally is, must give way that the true Ego can express, and when we speak of the ego we are referring to that part of the Self which functions exclusively in the physical self and in the external world,

You long for this. Patience is the need it is of vast importance.

Without it, nothing can be accomplished.

November 6, 1975

When the mind is deeply still, the Truth is there to express. Relax and let no thought enter other than that which is now flowing, unobstructed by the old limitations. Do not doubt. The very simplicity of this is filling you with wonder. Truth is always within reach and need not be struggled for. Become as a little child and receive it.

You are beginning to understand the importance of these communions. Their value is to help you orient your conscious being to the invisible world of spiritual Reality.

November 9, 1975

Do not condition these sessions. Again we say let the Truth flow. At last Man will be educated in this field. He will be taught to listen and obey. Thus God's will can be done on earth as in heaven. There is no other way. Be still and know that I am God. This has no meaning unless acted upon in absolute faith and acceptance.

Man will taste of these waters—not only the few but the many.

Radiance is the key word today. This very moment overflows with radiant good, even as the Fountain shown you in vision—the Source reveals itself in the radiant waters. You have hesitated to accept the full application given you for that purpose. You, all created beings, are the radiant waters, flowing forth eternally from the one Source. Do not separate the waters from the Source. Do not separate yourself from God and put Him infinitely beyond your knowing. It is not so. I am here and now as yourself. Do not insist upon this separation. You are the waters and I the Source even so axe we One and the Same. One cannot be without the other.

Now treasure this Truth today, deeply. It is enough for the present.

Amen.

November 10, 1975

Much has been said in these sessions: if you would absorb the last communication transformation of consciousness would take place. The message of the Fountain is so simple, the symbol so eloquent, so complete. The invisible is made visible through the shining waters.

Man's tendency is to separate himself from his divinity. He feels himself unworthy of such a holy Truth.

The purpose of these quiet times is to establish the absolute union of the soul consciousness with its human instrument. Revelation is the realization of this Oneness. There is no separation, save only in the form. This is the great step forward for you today. Until you are established in this Union you cannot be fully used, for all depends upon it.

November 11, 1975

What you are doing is drawing from the invisible you the Truth of your being. It is the most important step of your present existence. This is the guidance you have been longing for. Do not let anything stand in its way, or break this rhythm More and more will unfold as your confidence is strengthened and you will rejoice that you have listened and recorded these morning quiet times.

Everything: all wisdom, all love, all truth, is within the Self—your Self. Therefore do not look to another, no matter how noble or wise. This only postpones your own spiritual maturity. It is, in truth, very simple to accept and the important thing to remember is that all spiritual endeavor must be steady and pure as a flame on a still night. Hold it so, do not waver. That is your weakness.

Your opportunity to fulfill your mission on earth is NOW. So be it. Consecrate the first hour of the morning to this work.

Night –

There is much to be accomplished; the night is far spent, the day is at hand. You have but to look, and the hills are white with harvest. It is a crucial moment on earth. The good is being garnered and used for the forward push of the whole. It is of utmost importance that this is understood.

Remember the story of the foolish virgins that were not prepared. They had no oil for their lamps and so they missed the bridegroom.

Be ready, be prepared that you miss Him not. O hear these words, for they are the pearl of great price.

Keep to your spiritual center within. Your tendency is to close the door after these sessions and forget. Picture to yourself this posture, your face turned inward in a listening position, that means an attentive and deeply quiet state. The human mind must be as still as a quiet lake in the dawn of day. No ripples, but only a gentle, smooth surface—waiting for the great event of the rising sun. Then picture to yourself the light of the sun rising from the horizon and pouring its energy, its life-giving warmth upon the waters of the lake.

These quiet times are the sunlight, the interior light of the Great Son, flooding your consciousness, immersing you in the spiritual afflatus that is life divine.

Be still and savor deeply this thought.

Later Night –

You have been placed in your present environment for this moment of spiritual growth.

You must take advantage of it because it is here, on earth, that this growth is possible.

Everything is conspiring to help you to center your consciousness on the Invisible One. These are momentous times. The wheat is being separated from the chaff. The winds of change, of the New, are sundering the old bonds and boundaries and garnering that which is ready for the great upward sweep of evolution.

Those whose hearts are open to the divine will be the nucleus of the New Humanity.

The Bridegroom cometh to claim His own.

Let these words which you are writing quicken your spirit.

The Divine is the only Real—Come closer, my child, Come.

The Christ has spoken. Amen.

November 12, 1975

The work is to be conscious all through the day. And when I say conscious I refer to the preceding analogy—the attentive state I described.

This is the leavening of the Bread of Life.

There is nothing new in this but the new cannot be established within Man without it.

Those who understand this are open to the New and will be in the forefront of the New Humanity.

But remember you are eternal and so it is necessary to have patience. Destinies unfold—they do not fulfill themselves in spontaneous combustion.

Everything is a part of the divine order.

November 13, 1975

You have observed how your faith in these sessions has wavered, despite our warning. You are continually judging by "signs following". We give you the Truth. We hold it up to the mirror of your mind. And then the old doubts, and lack of faith in yourself, obscure the reflection.

A still lake, a quiet steady flame is needed, day after day after day—and not only during these communions.

What you are doing now is building, in the invisible world, a strong foundation. This is necessary. Without it there can be no channelship. You understand this. So again we caution you to watch your thoughts, your attitudes during this new day before you. And hold to the Presence within; it is Real and your only Self.

And so go forth and be that which you are in Truth—a divine reflection of the One Divinity—God.

This is a sacred trust. The "Word" made flesh—even as your God spoke it to you.

"Being is the Word made flesh". Being is yourself, here and now. Do you see this? How could now be other than now.

"Now is the day of salvation" has no meaning unless this is accepted as fact.

For the first time you are recording what you hear from the voice within. This is of immense importance. These lessons, or truths are not coming from an entity outside yourself but from Light within your Self. Cherish them as such.

They are deeply personal to you. Guard them as sacred.

November 14, 1975

There must be careful and continual preparation for any transcendental experience. The spirit can express, fully, only through that which is transparent. The instrument must be cleansed of everything but the deep affirmative attitude that God is the only Presence—the only Reality.

The purpose of these lessons is to show you your Self. This Self is receiving, eternally, the full power and plenitude of the One which is its Source.

Therefore, affirm your wholeness—all suggestions of lack, such as a feeling of "longing" or a sense of loneliness, or failure or regret—these emotions deny your "wholeness", thereby obstructing the spontaneous flow of the waters of life. Remind yourself of "The Fountain" and its symbolism. The vision was given to you for this purpose. It cannot send forth both bitter and sweet water at the same time.

Spiritual maturity is an absolute necessity at this time. Childish dreams and playthings must be put away. You understand this, so listen constantly to my Voice. To miss this opportunity would be a tragic loss to you. You will miss this moment if you look elsewhere, or to another for your Truth. Your spiritual mentor is within—your tendency has been to seek in books or in others for your inspiration.

November 17, 1975

These quiet periods are the "open door" you have been praying for. Now meditate on this.

You must understand that the Light of Truth within the soul is God. And needs no effort on your part to enlighten the human mind. The human mind has only one function here and that is to be silent and let the Truth flow into it. All Truth comes from the Christ or the divine Light within the Soul. There is only One Christ—or the Eternal Son of God—who speaks wherever there is a suitable channel. Trust in Him—for He is the love of God, the Father, ever enfolding you, and all. Deepen your silence that He may enlarge these lessons and flood your conscious being with His marvelous nearness.

November 18, 1975

Listen, we say. Listen throughout this new day. Amen.

You are beginning to feel a sense of spiritual well-being from these periods of listening and you are realizing that this poise, this sense of inner peace is not dependent on anything outside your self. This is good, and productive, for this is the essential soil for the flowering of the spirit here and now.

This is the "maturity" which we require, that you may receive that which is prepared for you.

In peace and confidence lies your strength, as the Psalmist tells you.

The new knowledge will open up unused avenues of expression. There must be an absolute communion between the so-called human consciousness and the Soul or Self, which is its source.

November 19, 1975

This Oneness will be the Organ of the New Consciousness on Earth.

Wonder and reverence must fill your consciousness. These qualities loosen the artificial barriers, or constricting boundaries that exist between the human, personal self, and the infinitely, impersonal Self, or Soul. Doubt or discouragement only strengthens these barriers, as you know. The secret is to be constantly sensitive to "the still, small voice" or the Divine, and its marvelous Reality and Presence

In Truth there is no boundary. The purpose of these communions is to reveal this to you.

Nothing separates you from your divinity save only your unbelief, and sense of a separate self. Give over that self to the Source. This is the eternal law. The waters flow from their Source and return to the Source, ad infinitum—meditate on this.

November 21, 1975

You are now beginning to understand the purpose and the importance of these periods of quiet communion—to establish a rhythm of listening and recording. This is the essential way of the New Age. Nothing is of greater importance.

Clarity is what is needed. Obscurities must be opened up to the Light, and that which is hidden revealed. As we have said new wine cannot be poured into old vessels. Your discipline must be to let go of everything that obscures this Light.

The heart must beat for God, and God alone.

There is no punishment in this, but on the contrary, therein lies the freedom that you seek. The burden is the small self that conditions your life's expression. Your desire is to be rid of it.

So let the "little foxes" go that spoil the vine, and it will bear fruit. The Truth is so simple, so beautifully simple and easy to understand.

November 23, 1975

Again you are questioning the Source of these recordings. Do not be confused; there is only one Truth, one Reality, one Now. There can be nothing artificial about this.

Be assured, God is not mocked. So let your intuition be the judge. All is flowing from the Higher Consciousness—the Soul. Let it flow, quiet the heart, and relax your hold. Stay with your Self from whence comes all life, truth, and love.

Do not obstruct this flow with doubts or fears.

The Christ is your true identity. There is *no* separation. This is the absolute unchanging truth. To realize this is the object of these communions.

There appears to be a boundary beyond which the human entity cannot go, *dare* not go. That is the only separation. The test is the willingness to give over that self, to be the selfless channel.

Our promise today is this realization. *I am here within.* Do not trouble the waters—do not break this rhythm, Let go and receive. Be still. I am speaking to *you.* I the *Christ.* I am holding you, lest you fall back into the shadow self. 0 my child, receive my Presence, my Love. Do not look beyond this moment for it is the living-truth enfolding you. You are beginning to feel this. Trouble not the waters, lest the veil fall again.

My poor child, you could not hold it—but fell back into the old consciousness. But let the blessing of this moment fill the heart. You sensed my nearness as never before. It will come again. This is the purpose—the test. Rest for today on this.

Amen.

November 24, 1975

Be at peace. You are not of the old world. Have faith, have faith; your future rests with me.

Yes, my child, as I said in the beginning of these sessions, the planet is receiving its chrism—its light from beyond. This, the dawn of a New Age, and the new humanity will be those whose hearts are attuned to this Light. You had a brief taste of the heightened consciousness which is the New Oneness.

This Oneness, experienced directly, will be the new consciousness and will transform human existence. The boundaries between old and new are being swept aside, and the old with all its limitations and conflicts will be known no longer.

We see into the heart of humanity, as it is. The core of a person cannot be concealed for all is an open book to the Self.

Perfection does not yet exist on earth, but this is the path, the way to the goal. There is no other way.

Those who are ready will be used in the New according to the pattern of each soul, each unique existence. Each will be used to create a new world, singly or in groups. The beauty of the whole is the important thing. We gather the wheat from the chaff and behold, the hills are white with harvest.

These quiet moments of listening and recording belong to the New. This is the way, to listen, to record, to act. Let the soul-direct in this fashion. It is your Self. There is no other reality. Turn your face to the New and the old, the past, will fall away. Do not look back, but keep the conscious being in the light. Thus you will experience the new birth you have been longing for. Let the beauty, the freshness and spontaneity of the new fill your mind-heart this day.

Amen.

November 25, 1975

The human consciousness is like a bud, a closed bud, whose heart is not yet open to the sun. But inevitably the sunlight will open it and how beautiful is the heart of a flower, when it opens to the sun. So it is with the human heart, or consciousness; it, too, is a beautiful sight when the Light of the Divine opens it.

Even as the bud of the flower depends upon the great lord of the sun, that it may open its petals and expose its heart to the light, so you, too, depend upon the touch of the great Son of God—that your being may open up to His love, and release its perfume, its' elixir.

Meditate upon this analogy.

Today is a day for assimilation, a day to absorb and digest all that has been given you during these communions.

A quiet heart, a serene soul and mind, holding within it the Revelation, this is what is necessary. All must be gentle, open, peaceful. Do not rush these periods of recording, do not be impatient. This only closes the door.

The old way was to plead, to importune the Divine. The new is an unquestioning Oneness.

You need only to silence deeply the mind-heart for the spirit to speak, to inspire, to direct, and to instruct.

This is the lesson for today.

Amen.

November 26, 1975

The human consciousness is like everything else on earth. It is, as we said, a seed consciousness at first, and then a bud, and then a flower whose petals open slowly, gently, silently.

You feel "locked up" in the bud, which creates a longing to open fully to the Light. This longing, this secret interior and continual pressure on the Self, gentle though it is, is the way of spiritual growth on earth. It is the influence of the Great Spirit on all his creation, calling forth His own, back to His kingdom. Again, we say, relax and listen to that Voice only."

I am calling you. This is my Voice. So we urge you to keep within hearing, within the Light, the Light of the Sun, the Son, and you will find your being unfolding into this New Day.

Be at peace.

Amen.

November 30, 1975

Strength is what you need, more strength on all levels. You must strengthen your faith in your self, the Self that is eternal and divine.

O my child, this is the hour, the moment for liberation, I our release from all that has constricted and conditioned this life experience.

Do not look to another. Do not strive to hold or repeat what another has said. Listen only to the One, here and now, your invisible Self.

There is no other for you. You have studied and read and saturated the mind with what others have found to be true. The time for this sort of gathering is over. Listen and record only what is flowing into your mind directly from the Source of your own Being. I AM—There is nothing else to discover. I am speaking to you from within your own Self-hood, created by Me for this purpose. I AM. There is no other. You understand this. It is a question of experiencing it deeply, in full consciousness. It will come. Love more. That is the only way. The more you reflect love the clearer is my reflection. Be Love, and you will find I Am you, and all will be as I will it to be, on earth as in heaven.

Later –

As you love, so does love draw closer to you. Love in various ways and from various sources. Do not contain it, but let it flow through you—out to others—to the world—to God. Love must flow. It is the great river of life, and like a great river it must flow out, out beyond to its Source—the eternal ocean from whence it comes. Though love is invisible, intangible, it is more real and solid than a mountain, for it is synonymous with life. Love is life, and life is love, and the two are one and the same.

Amen.

December 1, 1975

As you turn to the Divine—I AM HERE. It is in the turning that is essential. That is the vitality of these sessions. You have turned about face—even as the prodigal son, "And while yet afar off, the Father sees and runs to meet His son". So it is with all children of God. The Light within is more luminous as you turn toward One. Keep your face, your being turned toward Me, your Christ, your spiritual Self all through this new day.And you will rejoice when evening comes, for all will have flowed, even as the fountain—from Me, thy God—to you, my child, and back to me. This is creative living.

It is so simple, so beautiful, so productive of peace and beauty and truth. It is the All. So do not let your Interest, your faith in these quiet times together fade or wane. You are equipped for these vital moments. Your sense of worship and wonder make the contact possible. You begin to feel my Presence, the stir of life within the soul, here and now.

It is so important to have this reality before the transition called "Death" takes place. It quickens your awareness of the truth that there could be no such thing as "Death" as suggested on the human level, but only life, forever, for I AM LIFE, and I cannot die.

December 2, 1975

Do not try and evaluate these words you are writing. Do not wonder about their validity, their worth. You have only to be silent, and I will speak. You have only to write what I put into your mind, and Be *Still,* be silent, be peaceful and expectant and full of the joy that comes spontaneously when I am expressing through you.

Always that which is true, which comes from the Higher realms, within, flows spontaneously, the human mind is the instrument. There must be the unobstructed unity between these two centers. The divine Consciousness within and the human instrument, thereby revealing the truth that you are not two but only one. This is the meaning, the purpose of the evolutionary life on Earth. This unity, this conscious harmony between the human and the divine is absolutely essential at this time that I may reveal my word. That the new heaven, the new Earth may be established. You have waited and longed for this moment of oneness—have you not? So be at peace, and rejoice that I am the power and the Presence directing these recordings. I reveal each day my instructions, strengthening your faith, your confidence in my absolute oneness with you, in the reality of my Presence, in my closeness.

It would be wise if you did not reread what you are writing, but simply let it flow, lest you are tempted to impose your thought here. The Truth is always a liberating force, while thoughts or conceptual thinking from the little self acts as a dead-end and have no power to liberate.

Remember this, and, again, let it flow.

You must express more love, not only to those souls who are lovable and akin to you, but to those who appear to be unlovely and alien to you. Understand this, for it is important. You must look out upon all life through the eyes of love, even as I do. You must not judge but leave all to me. Remind yourself constantly this day that I AM seeking this unity with you, even as you are seeking Me. This is the new revelation, this absolute union. And only this can bring the New World into being. All is being quickened, for the Hour has come. The New is the only real. Do not look back or strive to hold onto the old. Heed my word. This is a warning, the old image must go—so follow thou me. I will create a new image—one that will reflect that which I am more perfectly.

Always the old must go before the rebirth can take place. You cannot be in the old and the new at the same time. Understand this and be ready. I am lifting all those who are ready into a new awareness of Me, of my living Presence here on earth. Unless the human self lets go this cannot take place.

Love of Me, thy God, makes this possible.

So go forth into this new day and be that which I AM.

Amen.

December 3, 1975

I speak through the heart center. It matters not whether you think of me as the soul, as the self, as the Christ, as your God. All is One. There are many names, but only One Self expressing through countless centers, even as the countless rays of the sun, raying out from their center, are, at their source, the one sun.

So do not question or try to put into a category the One who speaks through these papers. I am—and that which I am is Truth itself is love. That is the Alpha and Omega

This question should not concern you so much. The important thing is to value these moments as dedicated to the highest you are capable of reaching at this time.

If it is Truth you are hearing, that is enough. It is the purpose and value of this effort.

Look at it as a preparation, a cleansing, a lifting into the New. All effort brings a response. These moments of communion are an effort to draw closer to Me. They cannot fail to flower into a greater realization of my Presence They are deepening this awareness. Those who are being prepared in the vanguard of the New Race must be listeners, the recorders of my ever-intensifying voice at this time.

I am calling forth my own to be the forerunners of that which is to come. So question not—but simply write as I dictate to you.

There is in truth only one you. This we repeat over and over. And so do not be confused between substance and shadow.

December 9, 1975

I speak through many aspects of myself, from the highest to the lowest.

The sun gives forth its light to its countless rays, even so do I shine on all that I have created.

The Christ is the Light—or my eternal Son.

Being is the Christ or the Word—and creation is the flesh, or the Word made manifest—but all, all is the Light of God, the Father.

There can be no channelship today without this deep understanding, that the Christ it Being, your being, your true Self or identity.

To be holy is possible, even at the human level, and this is the purpose of life—to be whole.

December 10, 1975

Human beings are like beggars—clasping their rags about them, refusing the robe and the crown and the scepter—*when* in truth they are princelings and their kingdom is my kingdom. But they refuse to accept their sovereignty.

In the New Age it will be more difficult for My Own to hide from me, for a veil has been lifted. So heed these words and accept the mantle of divinity which I place upon you—the experience called "Death" does not necessarily bring you into my kingdom, for this step must be taken here on earth. That is the important thing to remember. The invisible must be made visible on earth as in heaven. The Divine must be released here and now.

December 11, 1975

Harmony is my law. There can be no creation without this law. You, all Mankind, are governed by this principle. Only children violate this law and must pay the penalty.

Maturity—spiritual maturity—is the mandate for the New World. That means all aspects of the self, soul, mind, and body, must be integrated and work together in perfect harmony.

Remember, life on earth is like a school. You are taught through experience. Do not be blind to the substance of your lessons and opportunities, lest you remain in the lower grades, and in your adolescence.

To graduate from this earth school is your deep desire. Therefore, aware: arise, and come up higher. That is my council for today.

December 12, 1975

Today you are questioning again these recordings. You are wondering whether you are not playing at being God! What do you suppose this phrase means—Be still and know that I am God!

The whole purpose of these communions, these moments together, is to reorient you to that place in your consciousness where God spoke these words. Human nature appears to be so FAR from the truth that to accept this. Truth as Fact is almost an impossibility.

This is understandable, as human beings live almost exclusively in the small human aspect of themselves. But, inevitably, the time comes when they must advance beyond the small and orient their consciousness to their interior Beings. As we have been emphasizing, these recorded communications are an effort in this direction—that you may deeply understand that your Being is the Christ, the Truth, the Soul, the Higher Self, or as the phrase suggests—God Himself, for I Am All in all! Being is the Word made flesh.

To deeply experience this axiomatic and fundamental truth may come in a flash or gradually, dependent upon the individual soul and its readiness.These quiet periods are a preparation for that experience.

The invisible is the only Real—for nothing can be Real that is not eternal. The material self is only a veil, an instrument, a mask, which has been necessary in the Old World, for to lay the mask aside and let the divine speak invited mockery and crucifixion in one form or another.

This will not be so in the New World. The mask will be broken and the Face of the Divine revealed.

To write what the inner voice tells you, as you are doing, has a two-fold purpose. It clarifies your self to your Self, and by impressing the subconscious, where the past is stored, it purifies it and wipes out the errors and limitations that belong to the old. Thus you are preparing the way for that which is to come.

This is not difficult to understand. Always remember the invisible is the Real—the matrix for the visible, the form. So what you are doing is bringing into the visible world the Truth which is within the subjective realms of being. This is the purpose of these periods. And the effect of this is far more important than you realize.

Therefore, it matters not what label you put upon these recordings. Only value them with your whole heart. Regard this opportunity as a sacred trust, a gift from the world of light and love.

The tragedy would be to turn a deaf ear to this and to stay in the imprisoned state.

All this was given to the world some 2,000 years ago, through the life and teachings of the Great Soul—Jesus of Nazareth. But how many have really understood his message? The time has come again to give forth The Teaching. The New Cycle will lift those souls who are innocent of evil into a New Realization of their true divine nature. The time is now.

Watch, I say, again I say, watch and listen and record.

I have spoken.

Amen.

December 14, 1975

The living Universe is filled with ever-higher intelligences. Some are influencing the evolutionary cycles of the earth—others the Solar System, and so forth on out into the great Beyond Man must climb this ladder. The new divine energies will draw from his potential that which will push him forward. To prepare those leaders who will be used for this work is what is taking place now. This requires deepening your communion with the spiritual worlds within, whence comes all force, all energy, all light, all life. There is no other direction to turn to for those souls who are ready to move forward. Man's being is infinite. He must turn his attention there where his creative powers lie dormant and can be utilized and given form.

There are many potential creative faculties within Man, waiting for the focalized light of his conscious awareness. To teach Man to utilize these interior faculties will be the education of the New. The value of these early morning sessions is to release potent energies that will awake that which lies dormant within you, thereby equipping you for the New Leadership.

Always remember that it is the light within that enlightens. In this way Man is self-enlightened. He enlightens himself, he is a Self-evolving entity. It lies within his power, choice, his will, whether to move forward, or to lag behind. You have chosen to move forward. The responsibility is great but therein lies the incentive for growth. It is the burden of the little self that crushes man. The stranglehold of this ego-self must be unclasped and the dynamic interior powers released. It is dangerous to both Man and his world to let the old condition remain any longer. Events are moving with greater acceleration to their climax, that this *unclasping* may take place. The present upheaval in the outer world is the effect of this unwinding.

This is a highly sensitized moment on earth. The birth, the entry of the Cosmic Christ into the earth's atmosphere took place at this time in the earth's history. It is the custom to celebrate that event at this time of year in the Christian world. But how many of you understood the chrismatic importance of that transmutation. It is of *vast* importance for those souls who are awake and attuned to these mighty energies to seek the deepest meaning of this evolutionary event. For from it man received the tremendous impetus to rise to his true identity which is the eternal Christus.

These communions emphasize this sacred truth. But unless Man understands this, the great sacrifice was in vain.

This cannot be stressed too strongly. It is the light of the Christ, which is the Love of the Father that is enfolding Man and lifting him out of the shadows. This light belongs to all mankind. It flows from the Cosmic Christ and was centered on earth, through the great sacrifice almost 2,000 years ago.

Again, a new evolutionary cycle is beginning for the earth consciousness and all those children of men who have felt and recognized this light, even in a small degree, are being gathered and garnered for the New Earth—the New Dispensation.

To understand this deeply, is the purpose of these communications. As we have repeated throughout these recordings, do not hesitate to identify yourself with the Christ, for He is, in truth, the only Self, the only Son of the Father. It is through Him that you will find your real Selfhood, your immortality.

December 15, 1975

Though you seem a very small separate self, though you seem to be very far from the Christ, in your little world, this is not so. It is He who is speaking, whose Being is your being, whose love makes it possible for you to love whose life is shared with your life. There is no separation, for I am here speaking to you through these thoughts, through these quiet times, that you may awake to met your Self.

Much has been written about "The Second Coming." So be it—the time is now. Meditate on this.

Later –

Remind yourself of the beauty of the dawn of the New Day, and center yourself there. Let this freshness, unmarred by human vanity, shine from you and round about you. Let it shine forth, and your bodily self will radiate it, and it, too, will be beautiful.

December 17, 1975

As we have said, this is a training period for you. We are preparing the way for a deepening awareness of all that is divine, both within and without. You long for a "break-through" for clearer seeing into my nature kingdoms.

Put your whole heart, soul, and mind on Me, and concentrate There is only me way, one truth, and one life. And I am that One. We have said to guard these papers as a sacred trust. There is a reason for this. The flow of the Divine through the human consciousness depends on the blotting out of the ego-self. There will be a right time to share them, but the time is not now. The purpose is to protect this intimate flow of truth. There must be no self-consciousness here. As we cautioned you in the beginning, there must be no me or mine. Your part in these communions is to be silent. You will be told when to share them.

December 18, 1975

The Light is flooding the planet, both within and without. This is a crucial moment on the earth and for those attuned to the new energies. The clarity, the brilliance of the light, both solar and in the interior worlds, indicate this. You are witnessing the acceleration of the New Birth. Let this light flood your soul—your solar center—that the old may be separated and destroyed. Give more time and place to this chrismatic movement. Let his light consume you, for It is a consuming light and will destroy all that obstructs its flow.

The earth is moving into a new celestial dimension, from which flow rays of light that have never before penetrated the earth. These magnetic energies are stirring up the old. All that obstructs will be left behind, to be redeemed in another cycle.

Because of these new energies flooding the earth consciousness, many can commune with Me, for I am here for those who have eyes to see and ears to hear. I am the divine voice in every heart, if they will but turn and listen.

Inertia must give way that the New Light may *cleave* through all old thought forms that restrict and obstruct. We repeat—spiritual inertia must give way at this time for nothing can hold back the great upward sweep of the evolutionary process which is *lifting* the earth into a new potential of spiritual growth. Take heed, my child—and receive this light. It is the hour before dawn. A new day breaketh.

Amen.

December 19, 1975

You are beginning to have more trust in these quiet sessions—to realize that everything is pointing you in this direction. The still, small voice is becoming stronger. There can be no falsity here. Truth is absolute, and cannot be governed or controlled by anything less than itself. Truth stands on its own truth, and creates its own true expression. In this way you can judge; are the thoughts that are flowing into your mind at these times true? That should be your only criteria.

As you are observing, there is an unusually intense light and clarity in the heavens, both by day and by night. This indicates the earth's celestial role and place in the Universe.

As we have stated this light will *consume* and cleanse all that lies in its path. That which can be used in the New Cycle will be cleansed—that which cannot be used will be consumed. You and your world are being swept deeper into its cleansing intensity. Remember it is a *consuming* light and like a two-edged sword, it will both destroy and bless. This is its power and its purpose.

Blessed are those who hear and who understand, for theirs is the kingdom of heaven.

Amen.

December 21, 1975

Deepen your stillness that only my Voice will be heard.

Remember always, I AM—what could this possibly mean but what it affirms. The present Presence of that which I AM—God. Be still and know do not be reluctant to affirm it, for even a faint realization of the absolute truth of this statement will dissolve immediately any confusion or anxiety or doubts. Man must awaken his divinity and release it into his present life, and cease relegating it to some distant and illusionary heaven. Everything must be brought into relationship with the Now—the Present tense.

I do not say—I will be—could it be clearer?

Concentrate on this realization, lest you hear a voice other than mine, which eternally affirms the one eternal truth—I AM

So be it.

Amen.

December 22, 1975

Heed my warning about listening to other voices. The world speaks with many voices. Keep your center, lest you be lured from the One by a false magic. You are committed to the New, to Me, thy councilor and thy guide. Fail not this mandate. Few there are, as yet, with this will, this perception. These few are greatly needed at this time that the whole may be lifted higher. It is of enormous important therefore, that you listen and record. Do not question, lest you be fainthearted. All truth is immediate and simple and uncomplicated in its self-expression. For you can say of Truth, as you can say of God—*It is*—and where It is, all Truth is present in its entirety. It is a question of unfoldment from that point outward.

Therefore, we caution you to be *patient*, to be faithful—to be ready—and do not let its immediacy and simplicity be a cause of doubt. Mankind still does not grasp this fact that the pearl of great price is on his own forehead.

Look no further, my child.

December 23, 1975

The divine is the only Real—as it alone reflects the One. The human body, with its ego-self, is unreal from that level. When you are centered in that part of yourself, and are not conscious in the higher Self, fatigue, sickness, death, and all human disasters appear to be very real. But they exist not in the higher realms of truth. Therefore, we are urging you to center your consciousness in the real—where I am—and where no evil can come upon thee.

December 24, 1975

At this time, the forces of light, of Love enveloping the earth, are intensifying. Turn thy being into them, for they are *resurrecting* forces that will lift mankind, or those children of men who are ready, into a potentially higher consciousness. Let your thought throughout this day be "Thy Will be done on earth as in heaven." Do not miss this radiant moment.

The disintegrating forces are also rife. Beware of them, lest that which you have raised up be torn down. It is a time to turn thy entire being toward the Christ.

This message is both a warning and an offering.

Watch, I say, and be still—and know I for the signs are many and are before thee.

Amen.

December 25, 1975

I have said—come closer, my child. Come, for I walk among you this day. Feel my Presence, for I am speaking directly to the heart of men. *I am God—I am Life—I am* the *Christ—I am thy Soul*—I am thy Self.

I am saying to all, awake! I am life eternal and am eternally pouring MY life into you. I give and you receive. *Only* Love gives of itself eternally, tirelessly, Receive my love, and like the holy fountain, let it flow back to Me that I, too, may receive, only to send it forth to you again.

The Christ is that Love. The earth is overlit with His Presence, for He is the great Sun, or Son-that shines upon mankind, that *all* may awaken to me the Father of all.

The children of men are like the seeds in the dark earth. Without the Son the life within the seed would not quicken and unfold. So it is with the heart, the consciousness of men. The spirit within quickens not without the love of the Christ pouring down upon it. Open wide thy Being this Day that thou mayst receive and rejoice.

Amen.

December 26, 1975

Though the outward world looks dark and full of conflict, despair not, for where *I am*, all is light. Lift, lift thy being into this light and let the dead bury the dead, lest you are drawn back into the shadows.

You will go forth into this dark day as a bearer of light, and this light will permeate every aspect of your day, down to its finest detail. All will work together into a great harmony. Have no fear. You will rest at night, with only gratitude in thy heart. So be it.

December 27, 1975

I am always within you. You have but to turn to seek me to love me. As you go forth into the confusion of the outer world hold fast to the silence within. Keep thy being separate from those forces that would attack and put down.

Stillness is of utmost importance, for all truth, all life flow from the deep stillness at the Heart of Creation. Within you is this Still Center. Abide with me theme and all will unfold without fatigue of confusion.

December 28, 1975

Know that I am the pilot that guides thy ship for I am all in all. Therefore, rest—for nothing can interfere with this outflow of life and love. Faith in me is thy strength and thy security. I brought thee forth into my eternal safe-keeping. I hold thee, I sustain thee, I love thee.

Rest with that, my child and be at peace.

Amen.

December 30, 1975

Each soul has its own particular note to sound in the great symphony of life. The clearer, the sweeter the individual note the more beautiful is the whole. Think of it in that light, and if each individual part each musician, keeps his attention on the great conductor, how much more harmonious is the result.

I am the Conductor of the vast orchestra of my Universe. And I know every instrument, every unit, and I listen for each individual note. For all must play his part perfectly, that the whole, the vast melody of Creation reverberate throughout my universe in perfect harmony.

Meditate upon this simple analogy.

Amen.

January 1, 1976

You can look upon this day as the establishing of a new life for you. From this point onward build into each day a New block that the foundation may be strong and will hold and resist the winds and storms of change that are blowing all about you. Stand fast in the eye of the hurricane and stir not from thy still center. The fury of this hurricane will increase, but fear not—it cannot touch thee in thy sanctuary.

The world is being torn apart. The building forces are gathering the blocks for the New Jerusalem. The New Barth. And the obstructive forces created by the great adversary are resisting, and are thereby creating the holocaust.

Stay close to Me, my child, and listen to no other voice. This is of the greatest importance, lest you be drawn into the destructive maelstrom. Remember, it is always a question of guarding the consciousness and keeping it unstained by the evil of the times.

This beautiful day is for thee and thy friends—that thou may rejoice and give thanks.

The human calendar offers a New Year. Let it be so, for the potential is there, within each of you.

Meditate on this.

Gather these notes into an orderly form and arrangement. The time is drawing near when you can share them with the few who understand.

January 6, 1976

In answer to thy prayer I say to deepen thy love for those beings of Light, invisible to the physical eye. You love to see them, these angelic and elemental beings, and my servers and messengers. They have no other will save but to do my work—my will. They belong to the sacred worlds of the spirit of love and beauty and will always be invisible to unregenerated man and beyond his reach. They are, therefore, uncontaminated and unstained by the profane world about them.

Those souls (and there will be an increasing number of them) who have the expanded vision and can observe and communicate with these beautiful forms of life have opened up the sacred centers within themselves necessary to project their consciousness to this kingdom.

You were given a glimpse of the etheric, creative inner realm through vision in answer to your earnest prayer. You were shown the forming the archetypal creation, of a flower, with its presiding elemental. You entered this kingdom by projecting your conscious being there, through love and reverence for God's world.

The new radiant energies permeating the earth at this time will aid in developing this expanded vision you seek. Nurture this truth and accept the presence of the beautiful etheric forms all around you, and sooner or later you will see them.

January 7, 1976

You are seeking a way to express thy new age ideas. To be an active part of the new culture. These communions are a "breakthrough" to the creative energies you seek. To listen, to record, and to act. This is the way. The first step Is to listen. To do this there must be no human unrest and arbitrary demands. I am here to direct, to instruct when the consciousness is deeply still and receptive. The creative potential is infinite. You must realize this and unite with this infinity within you. It will dissolve all old thoughts of limitation, both conscious and unconscious. There are, as you know, many levels of Consciousness to permeate—to cleanse. As we have emphasized old egoistic thought patterns must be broken up, in order that the new may be released.

The New is a vast magnetic field of ideas, draw upon it. These creative forces are irresistible building forces and will seek the essential avenues necessary to express through. Each soul is a unique channel for that expression.

Give yourself to those forces today, and you will be both used by them, and will use them for your own particular and individual expression.

The new knowledge, the new vision of the Universe around you will inevitably unfold, through spiritual and cosmic laws. Revelation takes place through consecration and concentration.

By listening and recording you are not only strengthening your own spiritual forces but are helping to establish and strengthen the foundation of the new Age on earth.

And so be at peace. You *are* being used—for this is the truth you *seek*.

Amen.

January 9, 1976

Yes, you understand that the "persona" or mask is no longer a necessary protective shield. The new education will be to draw out the divine qualities in man. That the soul may be unmasked and, express more freely than ever before. When the many will understand this, great souls, great beings, can come to birth on earth and guide mankind into the new dispensation. They can come and not be mocked or destroyed.

The masses ever long to be led. They are like poor sheep and will follow any catalyst, be he holy or satanic But Satan has had his day on earth. He has accomplished and is accomplishing the destruction necessary to open the way for the new to enter.

To unmask the Self is the purpose of evolution on earth and the purpose of these quiet communions together.

January 9, 1976

Yes, you understand that the "persona" or mask is no longer a necessary protective shield. The new education will be to draw out the divine qualities in man. That the soul may be unmasked and, express more freely than ever before. When the many will understand this, great souls, great beings, can come to birth on earth and guide mankind into the new dispensation. They can come and not be mocked or destroyed.

The masses ever long to be led. They are like poor sheep and will follow any catalyst, be he holy or satanic But Satan has had his day on earth. He has accomplished and is accomplishing the destruction necessary to open the way for the new to enter.

To unmask the Self is the purpose of evolution on earth and the purpose of these quiet communions together.

January 25, 1976

We have stated that the One expresses through a Hierarchy of countless centers of light. Therefore it matters not what name you give to that which is flowing from the interior, inner world of self. Call it simply The Truth Speaketh.

January 21,1976

Be still and write, and the answers to your questions will unfold. All is under Divine control. You have a tendency to forget this and when that which you, as a human personality, have envisioned as the answer does not materialize as you had expected, you become disconsolate and negative.

What everyone on the Path must consistently live by is "Not my will but Thine be done," even to the end of earth life. And remember, that which you are, in Truth, is invisible to you, which brings into play the vital necessity for Faith. Through this quality of Faith, you are now striving to reach this one, invisible to sense perception, through the intent and will to let this One be the guiding Light.

This means keeping thy face, or attention, turned inwards throughout the day—listening. If the voice you hear speaks to you of Joy, of Love, and a New Birth, you are listening. If you feel impatience, resistance, discouragement, you are listening again to the small human self, and so you will out picture these moods.

This is the answer to your question of why you seem at times to be in the old consciousness.

We have emphasized this from the first moment of these communications. As we have so often pointed out, it is not an easy discipline to follow; but no disciplines are easy, and the more valuable and precious the treasure, the goal, the higher the price.

To give over all self-will and egoistic pressures to the *Invisible One*, not in part and at certain intervals, but *con-*

tinually and at all times is the price for this goal.

All spiritual life is one whole, a continuum of light or truth and cannot be fragmented or isolated in compartments here and there.

As we have said, he who has been given much truth, much is expected of him.

Fail not, then, for intuitively thou knoweth, that the fruit of Truth is always sweet to the taste, but does not fall easily into the hand, it must be reached for with all the ardor and strength and will of the soul.

January 25, 1976

Your earth existence has threads running through it of many colors, some clear and beautiful—others not. We are interested only in the clear ones, especially the one that outshines all the others—the gold ones. The love of truth that you have pursued throughout the years. This thread has led you inevitably to these moments of communion. It has dominated the interweaving of the tapestry of your life. It is of great Importance that you use only this one gold thread to finish the pattern of your present incarnation. It will shine out and lighten the darkness ones that cast shadows in the harmony of the whole. You understand. We tell you this to strengthen your resolve, to steady your objective. To listen, and to record, and to Act, is the way of the thread of gold.

January 29, 1976

Your mind must not be busy or intrusive at these periods. But, as we pointed out, it must be as a polished mirror that we can reflect upon it our instructions—that we can speak directly to you. There is great magnetic power in these early morning hours.

The night is far spent, the day is at hand. The new day on earth. Therein lies a vast new reservoir of creative power. To draw upon this reservoir is the privilege of the few who are open and ready. And have been prepared through long years of self-discipline. These energies must be safeguarded lest they be mishandled and used for purposes that build not the new. You understand this. But your tendency is to be impatient—to want immediate action—specific plans and objectives. This is not the way for you at the present time. As we have stated in the beginning of these sessions, the purpose is to prepare you for the role which lies ahead in your spiritual destiny. These communions are the beginning of that preparation. Be at peace and rejoice that this is so. A vast and glorious destiny rests on this preparation. So be it.

Amen.

January 30, 1976

It is because you long for Me and love Me that I can speak directly to your mind and heart in this fashion. I use the contents of your mind—your vocabulary, that you may understand the simplicity of this sort of communication—the absolute unity. It matters not what words I use—whether they are very simple or very complex. The essential thing is communion. You are now becoming one-pointed. And that is the overall purpose of these recording periods. There is a change, a very subtle change in your conscious awareness of me—already, although in point of time as you understand it, this experiment is but a few months old.

This is the way—the way of the "Second Coming" of the Christ on earth. Direct communion and at Onement—releasing the divine will on earth as it is in heaven. For the two must be made one. This direct influence of the cosmic on the human, individualized soul will change the world into the New Heaven and the new earth. For man is ready for this. Suffering prepared him, and will prepare him for even now he begins to sense that he has wandered far afield and has lost sight of his Father's house. These are the signs of the times.

The better part of your present life has been turned toward Me, and that is why you are now being prepared for a role in the leadership of the new humanity. You ask what will be that role and when. We repeat, this must be left in my care, for only I can see the road ahead, and your readiness to act, when instructed to do so by

Me; and so be at peace—and listen and be attentive to my voice which is ever speaking in your heart. Do not look for the spectacular—a pillar of fire, or a personalized Christ in your midst. The Second Coming will not repeat that which has been. But His Voice will be broadcast throughout the world for those who are ready and who belong to Him and the new Revelation.

Amen.

February 1, 1976

It is enough for the present. You must absorb and savor deeply all that you have written. A transformation of consciousness is the objective.

Sometimes silence speaks more eloquently than words. Deepen this silence, but let it be as a flame in the "now" and not as a remembering. I speak through the silence as well, for I never forsake thee. I am that Silence as well as the Voice speaking in thy heart.

Rest, I say, for the present—in that deep and living Silence. Meditate there, for within this stillness burns the fires of revelation.

Amen.

February 2, 1976

You are still doubtful, at times, of the Source of these transmissions or recordings. A breakthrough does not necessarily mean that the human channel, or instrument must be perfect, or a saint or master. The only requisite necessary is that the mind which is offered be dedicated to the search and love of spiritual truth—for the mind-heart is the instrument.

It is, in one way, a dual operation, consisting of both creation and cooperation. For the vocabulary, the speech, the words are yours, but the Truth, the substance of the messages, as they form within your mind, flow from the higher world of the spirit.

The basic need is an instrument lovingly put at the service of the Divine and the more open and lucid and dedicated the mind is, the more spontaneous and immediate can the Truth flow through.

We have said these communications come from the Light within your Self, and from no other.

Although often the pronoun "we" is used, it is simply indicative of the universality of Truth and Love. All communications from the Higher Self to, or through the human-ego, or lower self, must be a fusion of this sort--for the purpose is to integrate the two into the Oneself--which is the Divine Ego or Son--made in the image and likeness of God.

February 6, 1976

It has been said—resist not evil. Therefore, once again we say—resist not the forces of chaos that are changing and breaking up the old world. You cannot stay the hand of destiny. The old must be broken that the new pattern take shape. Leave the shape of things to come to me. Your work is to build with me the new earth. By that is meant to stay within your center of light. It serves as a beam, even as a lighthouse on a rocky shore. This is your objective. To beam out into the chaotic world of men the searchlight of truth, of justice, of harmony.

This is the divine way to overcome evil. Always replace evil with truth. This is the healing of the nations, as well as the healing of the human body.

In this way you become a part of the new leadership. The new humanity, and also a part of the vast hierarchy that rule the planet, and beyond.

Amen.

February 7, 1976

Again we say, the work, the discipline is to center your whole being in the living, dynamic Now, for it is here that the vitalizing and fructifying power is concentrated and can flow forth into thy present existence. It is here, as we emphasized, where the light beams out into the world and beyond.

This is the test that we ask of you, and it is the highest and most difficult task that could be assigned to you, for the self longs for external activity that will objectify itself. This is not the way for the present, for what is needed is a still, open, conscious channel through which the light may penetrate and be focused for the good of the whole.

This has been our message to you from the beginning of these communions. The "signs following" must be left to Me. Your work is to be the selfless channel. The small self always resists this discipline.

Therefore, heed our warning and be awake and aware at this still center. The living Now. And ask for nothing else at this time.

We have spoken to you in these communions of the power and the presence of the interior self—the One invisible to the external world. But the One who reflects the infinitude of Truth itself and have repeated many times that the purpose of these communications is to reveal to you that Self through which God speaks and moves and has His Being.

Amen.

February 16, 1976

It should be evident to you that a form is taking shape. A form through which will radiate the new energies, energies that will increasingly reflect my Presence, my Oneness my Voice. When Man becomes such a center—alone or in groups—a nucleus is formed, much as a radio station, through which can be broadcast the forces that will enlighten and enlarge man's Consciousness of Truth. You have only to look, out upon your immediate world to see how such a center or broadcasting station is of vital importance. This is what we are asking you to be, and as your understanding of this and your effort becomes steady and steadfast, the result will be more widespread and effective. Hold, we say, to this discipline. It will have far-reaching results and the fruits will be sweet to thy taste. As this light floods your consciousness, it beams out, as we stated, and you become as a lighthouse on a dangerous reef. And so are lives saved and God's work established on earth as in heaven.

Amen.

February 17, 1976

I spoke of a form that is taking shape. It has been said "where two or three are gathered together in my Name, there am I in the midst of you" and so it is. And so it was as you shared these papers with the two who are of the light. Thus the nucleus is widened and strengthened. And the light becomes more forceful. This is the plan and for this we are preparing you. As we have said from the beginning of these sessions, the way will unfold and clarify itself. But without the necessary discipline and patience the form will not take shape. Understand this and keep thyself one pointed and all will be as I will it to be, for love is the projection of this light and this plan.

February 18, 1976

Only as you absorb into your being the forces of light can you become equipped for leadership. Only then can you contribute to the New. This is the purpose of these communions—that the plan may unfold. As you dedicate yourself to Me and My Will you become, as we have repeated, a center, a radio—magnetic center, if you will—where the power can be focused! This is not difficult to understand, but it requires both faith and patience as this dynamism is invisible to you at this time. The New Epoch on earth will be one of wholeness, where man at last will be integrated and no longer fragmented. This will not happen overnight, but the first signs of things to come are becoming visible even now for those who have eyes to see.

We have been emphasizing this all through these communications.

It has been said, Man does not live by bread alone. The implications in this utterance must become a reality. The substance must be released in the world as living Truth for such it is.

Amen.

February 23, 1976

You must watch your reactions to events in your objective world lest "the little foxes spoil the vine". The small self, the human ego is ever ready to grab the consciousness and be master of yourself. This is the "Pandora's Box" of all evils as you know. The purer your Conscious Awareness of Truth the clearer will be the gulf between the two and the more obnoxious will appear the small self as it "rears its ugly' head" so to speak. Thus it is less difficult to correct your human reactions and return to the purity of your Being. This is the discipline expected of you. "Do not fail for that which has been built up can be leveled again in a trice unless you are watchful and one pointed, as we have cautioned you.

You must look out upon all through the eyes of love, regardless, as we have emphasized. Criticism, judgment and unloving thoughts must not be allowed. This is a warning. And of utmost importance for the Divine cannot lodge in a consciousness that vibrates with emotions other than love.

As we have explained to you, separation, fragmentation obstructs the spontaneous flow of the life force, which is truth and love. All spiritual growth and unfoldment depends upon this self-discipline. This is not difficult to understand but needs only a watchful eye and careful vigilance. -And remember the ego mind is like a sponge and absorbs all emotions and reactions in order to express them in one form or another in the objective world.

If you read over these papers, you will see the tremendous importance of this warning. So be it.

Amen.

February 26, 1976

We have warned you that if you let yourself be drawn into the confusion of the outer, the old world, you must pay for this in kind. We understand the temptation. It is a natural reaction. But as we have pointed out to you, this does not aid in the transformation of the old to the new. Nations as well as men must live as *one whole* under God's will. The nation within which you have incarnated will emerge purified and reinstated in the natural order—but no longer a separate entity. The new earth consciousness will integrate all nations into one whole fabric, safeguarding their individual colors in the interweaving pattern of the whole.

The construction of a New World rests on new knowledge, new ideas, new energies. To resist the change is to hang on to the old.

The infusion of these new divine ideas into those who are chosen will be the leverage that will lift the earth into the New Dispensation

We repeat, keep thyself in thy Self—a Fragmented consciousness cannot be of use.

Later –

You will see as you look over these papers there has been one theme and that is the oneness of all life. There is- only on one God, and one Son who is the eternal reflection of the One; upon this divine fulcrum all Creation rests.

Take heed and go not back to the old fragmented world. As we have emphasized the life force is Truth and

Love and must not be obstructed, but must flow freely throughout the Universe.

We urge you to listen deeply to the voice within you and to no other. It is guiding you away from the old and into the new. Understand this.

Later Night –

As your consciousness expands into a greater realization of Me as a living Presence, so do you feel an intensification of love flooding your being. My love is always gentle and tender and fills the heart to over flowing with a peace that passeth all understanding. You are feeling this elixir. When this takes place, where are your doubts, your questions, your fears? They exist not where Love is. This quietude, this gentle awareness of my Presence is the good fertile soil for spiritual growth and flowering.

March 1, 1976

All will be made clear to you, depending upon your trust, your faith and obedience.

Because of the urgency of the times, the spirit is quickening, those centers through which it can speak and work that the new may be safeguarded and established.

The human part of the human being is like a child and must be disciplined and taken by the hand and led.

This is what we are doing. There is, as you know, a vast host or Hierarchy of beings of Light who are helping in this task. The Christ is the voice speaking through this Hierarchy.

We need only a dedicated heart which has been opened to the spiritual world of truth.

We repeat, the world of men and the dangerous environment which he has created necessitates accelerating our effort to establish the new energies lest the planet be plunged into utter darkness. If you read over these notes you will realize how important it is for you to stay within your center, your self, your sanctuary and do not try and salvage the old. As the plan unfolds you will rejoice that you have listened and recorded and acted as we direct.

Amen.

March 5, 1976

You ask why the earth is so important to man's spiritual growth. It is because the earth holds all within its bosom as seeds, including man's divinity. The fullness of everything is enfolded within its particular genetic seed and therefore must unfold here where the seed has been planted. As the seed of divinity within the consciousness of Man becomes quickened and begins to grow as a flower grows, as a tree grows from their seeds, so does Man no longer have to remain enclosed by earth as his soul opens up to the light, to the higher energies of the spiritual worlds He rises from the earth consciousness to higher realms of being. That is why he must turn to the great Son, as we have stated—that his soul may be opened here—that the earth fall away from the seed consciousness and the flower emerge. There is involution and evolution, a winding up and an unwinding, as the consciousness is immersed in the light and the love of the great Son of God, the truth of being, of all being, unfolds.

The natural world holds within it the secrets of the Universe The seed holds within it the whole. The infinite is within man and must unfold. That is the divine plan and the divine purpose of life right here and now, on earth as in heaven.

The new cycle is bringing new energies of light and truth to further the quickening of the consciousness of man—that he may grow and rise from his present imprisoned state—his present earth consciousness. You have absorbed this truth and are therefore open to the new energies. That is why these communions are possible. Verily, verily the seed is the Seed of his Goodhood and he must nurture this Seed that his true being may be released.

The soil in which the seed is planted is faith in Me thy God. I am calling-forth my own and those who hear will rise into a greater flowering Into the light of a new day.

I call "my own" those who know intuitively this truth and therefore the spirit quickens and answers my call. For the spirit within Man is the Christ Consciousness or the spirit of Love and Truth.

Amen.

March 7, 1976

When we speak of the Christ, the Great Son of God, we speak of the spiritual Essence within man which is enfolded deep within the Being of the individualized self. This Christ Self is both within and without, although in truth there is no within or without. This Self is the reality that all seek on earth, no matter what words or names are coined to express this Essence.

When I say, I am calling forth "my own", I am calling forth this Divinity within Man—to awake and rise up and return. This Truth, this Essence has been incarnated and embodied on earth in various degrees of expression during epoch after epoch in order to arouse Man from his long sleep, and like the prodigal son, return to his father's house. But Man still confuses shadow for substance. The substance of Life is always divine Truth and Love, and all that is derived from these two. What men have built up on earth belongs not to Truth or Love.

March 8, 1976

The difficulty of accepting the full awareness of the divine source, of these recordings lie in the conditioned mind of the small self. This self is conscious only of its enclosed boundaries and therefore cannot soar beyond into that which is timeless and spaceless. For the most part, human life takes place within these enclosed boundaries and few dare step beyond.

We are asking you to step beyond. This requires, always, a tremendous faith and understanding, as well as an unwavering love of divine truth and its dictates, which is the way to that which is spaceless and timeless. Without this love and understanding the door to the Beyond remains forever closed. If your love for that which is unfolding here and now, falters, the door will swing back again and you will be left within the enclosed boundaries of the small self. This is why we are constantly urging you to meditate upon all that has been flowing through your mind at this time. There is always the Adversary waiting to destroy truth and tempt the self back to its conditioned world. This is the way of death and not of life everlasting.

Heed our warning, my child, and listen only to the Divine Voice that is guiding you through the open door into the new and away from the old conditioned world, which has enslaved the soul of men.

This open door is within thee, and it is here where I am Calling thee.

Oh fail not this hour—for the dawn breaketh and a

new day is before thee.

It has been said only the pure in heart shall see God—the pure in heart are those whose hearts are centered on Me, thy God—and wavereth not.

Amen.

March 9, 1976

Hold to the love and wonder that stills thy heart when it listens to the voice speaking within it.

It is easy to push this still small voice aside and listen instead to the voice of the world. The world-self is an entity, an amalgam of forces built not upon truth, and therefore to survive it must repudiate truth. Its cry is "crucify, crucify"—for it mows that Truth will destroy its sovereignty—and so it will.

Heed not this voice. It will obstruct the divine purpose unfolding within these communions. It is the voice of doubt and unbelief and ever mocks the purity and innocence of the unworldly. We caution you constantly for the danger is always at hand—like a dark shadow.

The Truth leads always towards the Light, for truth and light are one.

Amen.

March 11, 1976

As we have said there is much work to be done and although the responsibility is great the results will be sweet to thy taste.

These communions are a preparation for that which is to come. Always remember the energies which make this communion possible are the New Age energies or vibrations and as such they are creative and transforming forces that are flowing from a cosmic or divine source. Therefore, old thought patterns of separation and limitation and unbelief must *not* be interposed here.

These creative energies that flow from truth and love will embody themselves perfectly in the objective world, if not interfered with by the conditioned ego.

To listen, to record, and to act. This is the way to the fulfilling of this plan that is taking shape—and *the* new way of life on earth. For once again, as in the beginning, the Divine will walk upon this planet.

March 13, 1976

The voice within, the voice of Truth, always speaks spontaneously. Let it flow. Do not obstruct it or interpose thy thoughts—and always remember the spirit of truth and love is ever impersonal and universal. Therefore, do not impose upon it the boundaries of the finite mind. If you judge these papers, these communications with the small, personal mind, you are looking out upon the spirit of life from the wrong end of the magnifying glass or telescope, so to speak. And doubt and unbelief will once more enclose the self.

Always start these morning quiet times with the great Prayer and relax thy hold on consciousness.

Be still. Be at peace with the glory of the dawn. I am the power and Presence enfolding thee—and all.

Amen.

March 14, 1976

I speak to thee from the vast realms of cosmic light and at the same time I am the still, small voice within thy heart. This is my will. Receive this light which is the new directive force on earth.

All that has been given thee in these pages flows from this center of light and are liberating forces to prepare thee for the necessary channelship at this time and place. Each individual who will play his part in this New Drama on earth has been prepared that each will add his particular contribution to the divine paradigm that is forming. This form that is taking shape here and now I will become a radiating center of the New Age ideas. As we have been emphasizing, this is the dawn of a new age and will therefore release the energies that belong to a fresh beginning—to the innocence and uncontaminated spirit of a young child. Look out upon the dawn on earth and absorb the rosiate glow from the rising sun. Let the freshness, the ecstasy of lifted wing and song fill thy heart with the elixir of the dawn of a new day on

Earth. Go forth into thy day with this joy unchecked in thy heart and all will unfold according to my plan. Where joy and love and truth abide in a heart, there am I. And therefore fear not. All is unfolding and will clarify itself as you listen and record and act.

March 17, 1976

We are gathering together the threads of gold in the tapestry of thy life that thy destiny may be fulfilled in this life experience.

Being is the Word Made Flesh.

All three are one and the same power or Presence. The "Logos" or "Word" *IS* "Being" made manifest or flesh. Spiritual Man, is all three in one. He is Being, the Word, and Flesh or Form. *That,* is why we repeat the Christ, or the "Word" is thy true identity. And that is why we emphasize the contemplation of the Being part of thyself. It is thy true Self and is not separate from the Universal One.

Because of this these communions are possible.

Later –

Always at the inception of a New Epoch on earth, there is a fresh influx of divine energies flowing from the universal presence of Truth and love. These energies are now operating on earth and are uncontaminated and untouched by the old. To keep them so is the objective we place in thy hands. Meditate on this truth.

Amen.

Night –

Fear not. Nothing can harm thee, can touch thee, can separate thee from the love that flows eternally from the Christ who is both with thee and within thee. Let his light encircle thy being, thy environment.

Feel His love and see His light shining all about thee. And where there is light there can be no shadows, no darkness. Fear not. As you call upon His Name so does He hear and answer, for He is closer than breathing, nearer than hands and feet, and there is no place where He is not. Rest in Him and be at peace, for he who dwells in the shadows cannot attack where there is the Christ light.

March 20, 1976

Let thy heart be at rest in the great silence wherein the timeless can *be*. This silence—this eternal now is where the divine coincidence takes place—where the human and the divine meet. It is here where these communions are taking place. The finite mind and the infinite can be as the holy fountain. The infinite gives forth its light, its truth, and the finite in turn releases it back to the universal.

As we have repeated in these recordings, the life force is truth and Love and must flow and never be held in a closed self.

Truth and love are the substance of thy being, for life *is* truth and love. As you receive, so must you give. Joy comes from the giving, the releasing of this elixir back to the universal, the *All*.

Again we say, deepen thy confidence in all that is of the Light—the Light that ever flows from the Christ—from the One. Look upon all that confronts thee, that challenges thee—not as evil, but as an angel in disguise, strengthening thy faith in the One truth, the One presence. The greater the challenge the stronger must be thy faith. There is nothing to fear, as we have said. Strength is what you must build upon. With faith in thy God, and the strength to keep it one-pointed, nothing can touch thee but the love and truth which is even closer than breathing. The Light overcomes and dissolves every shadow no matter how fearful it may appear to be. Rejoice in the glory of the unfolding divinity all around thee. Taste with thy soul the uncontaminated freshness and beauty which is awakening in the nature kingdoms. The young new leaves and blossoms are symbols of the resurrecting principle that stirs the heart, and soul to *lift* up and awake from its dormant state, and realize that this is the divine ever calling to all creation.

Drink of this pure water that overflows from its living Source—the great Heart and Soul of all Cosmic life.

Shadows may lurk behind thee, but the light even shines upon thee and before thee.

Fear not—and press on and never falter for where there is love in thy heart, nothing can overshadow thee.

March 29, 1976

Simplicity is the necessity. The absolute immediacy and nakedness of truth. Do not struggle to enrobe it with old thought forms. To clog the heart with past images and attributes only obscures the flow the unsullied light that enfolds all in its transparent purity. *Dare* to stretch forth thy heart to Me as though new born—untouched and unstained by the *imprint* of passed centuries. *Be* newborn, even as an infant comes forth into the world nakedbe thou unclothed with the doubts and timidities that belong to an old and dying world.

Stand alone and naked before thy God.

There comes a time in the history of a human soul when she must shake off the dream of otherness and separation.

The time is now.

Truth speaks with one voice—one will, one love.

Ponder these things in thy heart today and wonder not, nor

Deny the absolute simplicity and immediacy of the truth which is

Speaking for I AM and there is no other.

Amen.

March 31, 1976

When we say "ponder these things in thy heart" we are urging you to reflect upon all that is flowing forth into these communications. Reflect and meditate upon the truths that Lie before you in the natural world. Meditate for example, upon the miracle of the great oak tree unfolded within its seed, its acorn. If the whole tree, with its massive branches and rhythmic cycles were not within the acorn all the sun and rain and warmth of earth could not draw it forth. So it is with Man—if the fullness of the Spirit of Christ, of God, were not enfolded deep within the Seed of his being the full divine consciousness could never unfold.

It has been said, Man is made in the image and likeness of God. To reflect upon this truth, with all its infinite implications is what is necessary.

What does "image" mean but the perfect reflection of the One who is eternally reflecting Himself in The truth within the soul of man, as in a mirror.

Amen.

April 2, 1976

When we speak of a center which is forming here we speak of the spiritual forces that emanate from the souls who have been gathered here, in understanding and cooperation. Love for the truth released into these communications and an understanding of the potency of their release is the fulcrum upon which this centered light rests. Without this understanding and cooperation there can be no center. For these individual energies flow from the heart—even as the truth and love embodied here flow from the great Heart of the Universal One. As we have repeated throughout these communions It is the Cosmic Christ who overlights the whole vast structure of the spiritual Hierarchy that rules this planet and beyond. Those who have been chosen for this particular grouping of souls are those who are in tune with this truth.

It is important, therefore, to act only in accord with these communications, and not in response to the personal Will. Let the love of the Christ be the guiding light. He it is who is garnering his own. Constantly dwell in His Presence and all will unfold according to His will.

April 4, 1976

To dwell in His Presence is to hold the consciousness pointed in the divine sanctuary of thy being and not in the flux and filteration of the outer self. Every effort to do this brings its reward in greater strength, and therefore greater spiritual poise and power. Understand the importance of this. The personal consciousness, for the most part, releases energies that relate not to this spiritual center, but only to the objective, phenomenal world. These energies are often negative, insofar as they are not building a strong subjective self, or spiritual nucleus of divine activity.

It is important, therefore, to constantly examine the directive forces thou art identified with. Are they constructive and inherently building forces? Or are they preoccupied with the old self, the old world. As we have emphasized, the important thing to remember is to identify and embody only the *new* energies of light, of love and truth. And thereby be an instrument of His Will and Presence. Remind yourself of this, lest you lose yourself in the small world of the egoself—with all its anxieties and unhappiness and limitations.

April 5, 1976

When I say—I Am the Light of the World—What does this mean? On the human level it means that the I Am is the light or life radiating out from the conscious being of the Eternal. And this light, this I AM has been given to man to realize in full, for I AM is the everlasting affirmation of life eternal.

This is the Seed within the being of all that is self-conscious. As this divine potential quickens and unfolds, man's true Selfhood will expand into the fullness of the universal I Amness.

Be still and know that I Am That I Am—has no other significance.

Understand this, meditate deeply upon this and all the activities of thy life will reflect this light, this truth, this life, for I AM GOD and there is nothing else.

April 7, 1976

The human mind is ever busy with its personal images. As the months, the years come and go there is, for the most part, only a shuffle and a reshuffle of these images gathered from without itself. This data, these accumulated mental forces are what men regard as thoughts. But this is not *thinking.* Only that which flows from the Living Reality within the soul of man is true thought, or wisdom or truth. For this wisdom or truth to flow the human mind, as we have emphasized, must be deeply still and receptive. This can be achieved only by a deliberate discipline and control. When this is accomplished, the human mind becomes magnetized by the inflow of spiritual power. It becomes like unto a magnet and attracts to itself the ever ready divine reality. This is not difficult to understand. You have only to be still and watch and wait upon this truth and it will demonstrate itself.

April 8, 1976

Self-giving is the way to the transformation of consciousness. As we have said, a complete turning toward the Invisible One is the divine necessity.

As thy love for this One deepens, as thy desire for Him, thy thirst, consumes all other desires, only then wilt thou have the courage to step into the Kingdom.

Only then will the door swing open that thou mayst enter.

April 11, 1976

Absorb into thy heart the resurrecting energies all about thee. These living energies are pouring into the earth, to awaken all that sleeps within the natural world. Absorb into thy being this ecstasy, this life force, this creative fire. It will consume that which encloses the self and liberate the new growth that lies dormant there. Let this life force flood thy being, thy world. It will strengthen and illumine.

Nothing stands still. All is alive and in perpetual movement, in creative joy. Fear not. The heartbeat is life Eternal. All is unfolding in the Eternal. Live each moment as a gift of the Eternal. Listen to the word which is ever sounding within thy Being. The word is the 'Christ—is Creation—is life Eternal.

April 22, 1976

Whence cometh love and beauty into the world—or song or laughter, or longing for the divine beloved.

Whence cometh compassion and courage, and the inspired Will to seek thy God.

To meditate upon these things is to reach out and touch Reality—is to savor the Essence within thy soul.

The calyx separates and opens and silently, softly, the flower unfolds.

Whose Hand is gently opening the petals, whose eyes are watching and adoring? Who brought thee forth to ponder these things—to see and wonder and reflect the truth—as a prism reflects the light.

The calyx opens and the flower unfolds.

Meditate upon this image—its message, its truth will open thy heart, even as the calyx opens, releasing its essence into the world of men.

April 26, 1976

The cosmic clock regulates the duration of the form, but Eternity is the home of the spiritual Being using the form. That is why we repeat so often the eternal Now—for that is where thou art.

Eternity is ever around thee—is everywhere present, for

The timeless, spaceless presence of life, of truth, of love and Eternity are one and the same.

I am the Eternal, and all that I am is Eternal. To practice the presence of God is to live in the Eternal. Man's outer life is conditioned by the clock but his inner life should flow with the Eternal, unbound by time or space or the inventions of men.

To feel thyself to be Eternal is to experience reality—the deathless state. To live in the Eternal *now* is to enter the stream.

April 27, 1976

As you write, as you listen and record, creation is taking place.

What is creation but Revelation. Truth revealed. The calyx opens and the flower is revealed. The heart center opens and from within that sacred sanctuary the truth flows out.

Let it flow, my child, and be still and the truth that is speaking will build its own edifice, its own form, that will harbor the shape of things to come.

To be a channel for that truth, that expression, is thy privilege now. So be it.

Watch, we say, and Pray, for the time is ripe and the harvest will be garnered for those who await the Bridegroom and for those who are prepared, and ready.

Amen.

May 2, 1976

The vibrations of the atoms that form thy body are, in truth, controlled by the higher vibrations that form that part of thy mind or soul that is functioning on earth. As the consciousness, the human mind, lifts and shifts its center of gravity from the body to soul, the higher vibrations or spiritual energies, become dominant, and the light or truth that is the substance of live shines in full force upon the form or body. When this light is consciously focused the body becomes once again harmonious and in balance and its natural equilibrium restored. The light of the soul harbors no imperfections but flows unobstructed and uncontaminated from its source, as the rays of the sun flow forth from their center of light.

In times of stress to be in command requires the discipline we have been emphasizing throughout these communications. If you constantly finger with thy mind the condition you wish to be free of, the law of truth cannot operate, for no admixture is possible here. *Truth* is absolute. To dwell in the soul is to wall off, as out of bounds, the stuff of the lower form from thy activating mind with its fears.

The form is but a fleeting phenomena. It has no substance other than that. When you identify the consciousness with the bodily defect that you wish to be rid of you are entangling its image with the power of your mind, and thereby strengthening its hold, its reflection on consciousness, and so, on the body. To be free of all that is alien to truth, the mind must be held steady and steadfast in the center or citadel of thy soul.

Understand this.

May 6, 1976

Remind yourself, in times of stress, that you are never alone. The human self, caught up as it is in a false sense of isolation and separation cannot realize that although invisible to it, the great wholeness of Life surrounds this self. This Wholeness the omnipresence of Life and Love consists of countless Centers of Light, ascending and descending. These invisible Beings are in essence, all one Light, One I Am. This Wholeness, this Uni-verse is a living testimony to the everlasting truth that I Am All in All—for that which I AM cannot be separated from the Whole, anymore than the sunlight can be separated form the Sun.

When you meditate upon this Truth. You have but to reach out with your prayerful heart and you touch Life in some responsive form-as there can be no place where Life or Love is absent.

To realize this is to rest in This Wholeness. Your effort should be to accept and rejoice that you all beings are an integral part of this Wholeness-this Universal Presence of Life and Love-and as the Perfection, Harmony, Balance—there can be no lack in this endless Reservoir of Life-for every being who reaches out to It—there is a response.

Be still my child and let this Life Force of Truth and Love flow freely unobstructed by the little foxes the little human fears that spoil the vine. To be whole is to fill the consciousness with that sense of Harmony, of oneness with all that is Divine.

Listen deeply, lest the old engulf you and draw you

back into the shadows of the ancient race mind, with all its concealed evil, ever at hand, ready to destroy and corrupt and pull down all that has been built up.

Constant vigilance is necessary to keep the consciousness strongly centered in the light of truth regardless of what the world of the senses is reporting.

May 17, 1976

It would be wise to reread and meditate deeply upon all that has been given thee in these few communications.

Even as water reaches a boiling point, so too, does meditation reach a saturation point, and Revelation then takes place.

But without the necessary fire beneath the water it will not boil. So it is with the Fire of Truth, unless it is held steady and constant within the mind, the barriers that enclose the Self will not dissolve, and the truth be released.

Therefore, keep thy lamp lit, that the shadows enclose thee not. There are many windows of the Soul, but only One Door that opens to where He stands and awaits thee.

Meditate on this in thy deep Heart.

Amen.

August 14, 1976

You are listening to me now as never before. My Voice which is speaking directly to you can now be heard all over the world, through different channels.

Salvation is now at hand, through Me, thy Christ. Listen, then Child of God as never before, and keep thy face turned toward me, that revelation can take place. For only through revelation will the old and dying world be wiped out from thy Consciousness and the world that God creates be seen.

"I Am the Way and the Truth and the Life". The Way to the New Birth, to the Resurrection and Atonement of all.

Release everything into My hands for this is the hour when the Bridegroom enters the Bridal Chamber and claims His Own.

October 24, 1976

Remember the symbol given thee in the vision of the Fountain of Living Light Fresh Life or Light ever flowing from its source-ever new, ever unstained and unconditioned by that which has been used and known.

Keep this symbol, and its spiritual meaning before thy mind-It is important at this time-for it will inspire thee to control thy mind from re-acting to old thought patterns of limitation and fragmentation.

Let the shining water flow unchecked and then move with them in spontaneous delight into new activity that will reflect the freshness that belongs to the dawn of a new day.

This will invite those Higher forces that will bring to thee greater power and understanding. Let the prophetic message of this symbol become the great reality of thy immediate conscious awareness.

That which has been given to thee, from the Higher worlds, can come into being only in This way.

October 24, 1976

When you are open and sensitive to the world of Truth only, everything around you will speak to you of the Divine, of Truth. You have but to have ears to hear and eyes to see. These living moments are aflame with Truth. Therefore, let not a second, an hour pass without listening, without seeing, for the Divine is the only reality.

These quiet moments in the first hours of the day belong to the Divine reality of your being. You are listening, you are recording the "still small voice" which is speaking from within your heart.

This is the Truth you are seeking. This is Cosmic Knowing. This is reaching out and touching the spiritual world within.

Your tendency is to belittle this effort, to shrug it off as of no significant importance and to look elsewhere, or to another, for your inspiration. Can you not understand that your own Inner Divine Self can be the only Source of that which you seek. There is no other for you in this respect, no matter how noble or illumined.

Therefore, we caution you to consecrate all your aspirations upon this sacred centre within your own individualized Divinity and slight it not, for the outward expression of the remaining years of this present incarnation depends upon this.

October 30, 1976

The wisdom, the Truth that is flowing to you from the Inner realm of Light must be more to you than a written page. Light consumes the darkness, the shadows. Unless this is taking place within the human aspect of yourself it is useless to record these sacred moments. When all is Light within the mind, within the heart, the door of the Kingdom swings open. Therefore ponder these words, "I am the Way, the Truth and the Life" or Light. Be still and know this.

There is but one Christ, though he is both transcendent and imminent, both within and without. For there is but one Son, the Eternal Light or Love of God, the Father, shining within all creation.

Absorb this, and let this Light flood thy being. For only then will you be ready and prepared for that which is to come. The purpose of these communications is to emphasize this, over and over.

November 9, 1976

Remember where thy love should be centered—Always remind thyself of the one within and in the spirit of "Thy Will Be Done"—go forth into thy day with an open heart and consciousness.

This will aid in preventing purely personal attachment or desire. There must be no attachment to either person place or thing. The New must be unpremeditated and unconditioned—flowing forth from the Divine within. The personal self, or ego, is ever ready to grab the inspired moment and manipulate it to its own size and dimension, remember this—It is a warning.

Amen.

November 11, 1976

As we have said, you must love impersonally. Your consciousness must know one supreme attachment and that is to God, to Christ, to the Universal Good. This is important to remember at this time for all depends upon it.

It was said some two thousand years ago, "Love the Lord thy God with all thy heart, soul and mind. This is first Commandment". When the individual self has given itself to this supreme Love, all else unfolds. It is so simple to understand, for it is God who, in his incomparable love responds and gives.

When the individual soul looks only upon the Divine Beloved, the human entity is blessed without measure.

My child, this is thy lesson for today.

November 14, 1976

As the day breaks and the light of the sun begins to suffuse thy world once more with its life giving energy and warmth, so it is with the dawning of the Son of God within thine heart. Let His glory rise and suffuse thy entire being this day. Let Him come alive as thy self. Each breath, each heart-beat belongs to Him.

This Christ, this Interior Son must rise each day, each hour, even as the physical sun is doing, spreading the life giving warmth of His Presence throughout thy day.

As the sun mounts the heavens and the mechanics of existence occupies thy thoughts and activities, remind thyself of this dawning, this elixir, to keep it ever present in thine heart is the discipline required of thee.

Remember this at the noon hour and when day is done, think on these things.

November 18, 1976

The deeper your stillness the more creative you will become. That is the great paradox. To be deeply still consciously still brings you into the Universal womb of creation. To let your mind, your consciousness dwell in memory, or desire or mundane thinking, brings you out of reality out of the Universal Light, and into the shadow world of illusion-You understand this, so strive to remind yourself, during the days activities, of this profound truth. Divine Reality dwells in stillness never in the flux of the phenomenal world-deepen your stillness your silence there in lies both power and creativity.

Remember the Fountain of Living Light—There was no sound as the waters flowed. This is your symbol is t o be kept before your inward being.

The danger is always to personalize to latch onto an objective attachment. This stultifies the flow of divine Truth. Let it flow impersonally

Amen.

November 19, 1976

To write, as you are doing is a tremendous aid in keeping you in the atmosphere of Truth, of Spirit—Without this effort, as you have realized, the moment to moment realization of your Oneness passed without your being *Aware* of it—*This Oneness* –this *Atunement*, or *Atonement*—is the *living* and vital Fulcrum upon which all rests –

It must become the Way—for it is Life—Life Eternal -There is no other *Way* or Life. Understand this—for this understanding is the Open Door to the Kingdom—*To be Conscious*—of *This Divine Coincidence* of the human with its divine *Counterpart*—is the immortality that must be accomplished here on earth—*while in the body of flesh!*

Therefore, to record this Truth as it takes place, is a great aid in stabilizing this Unity—this Oneness, and we repeat, as it takes place—here and Now. This is the purpose of the quiet moments in the first hour of the day.

Therefore, let this Truth be—the *dominant note* of thy existence—let it be sovereign in thy Consciousness throughout this day.

Amen.

November 20, 1976

Although you, as a human entity, cannot see it, the direction of your life has already taken a *New Turn*—you are now traveling a *Higher* road than ever before. You understand, to some extent, the preparation that has been accomplished –for the more *drastic* change which is *at hand*—and that is good—Absorb all that has been given thee.

This release of the Truth from within the Sanctuary of thy Being—has brought to thee those Forces of Light that were needed to fulfill thy particular mission on earth at this time.

All is now under Divine Control—Rejoice that this is so—and be at peace.

Amen.

November 21, 1976

As we have stressed all through these papers, patience is the great need and absolute Faith in your divine self. Also a vigilance that the small self, the ego does not usurp the consciousness.

The purpose of these recording periods is to prepare you, that you may be of use—an open channel is what we need—that the higher forces may flow through. From the beginning of these sessions we have emphasized this in various ways and through various symbols.

To lift the heart and hold it steady in the light where the powers of the Christos are centered this is your place, as we have said. Hold it steady as a flame on a still night. There is no other way to bridge the distance between the unreal and the real the eternal and the temporal

Amen.

November 22, 1976

Do not try and plan your unfoldment. Do not be impatient and grab hold of these quiet periods with your human mind—Your task is to be serenely confident of the sovereign power that is guiding you. As we have said, the ego is always at hand to interfere with the divine, to take the inspired moment and manipulate it to its own size and measure. The voice of the ego is loud and aggressive, while the divine speaks always with a *still*, small voice.

Therefore it is necessary to cultivate the quietude, the silence we speak of so often.

Be still, and know, this is the Way.

Over and over we urge you to *Let* it flow. Watch and wait.

Creation of the New ever flows from the unknown moment.

An undisturbed and open heart is the absolute necessity—*dedicated* to the Divine, *trusting* in the Divine.

This is the Path.

November 22, 1976

Inspiration and Vision are a vital part of the New Consciousness for these qualities flow from the Divine, and they will invite Cosmic consciousness.

Therefore hold to the inspired Vision of a New Earth—a New Humanity at One with God and all Life A Humanity attuned to the Universal Brotherhood of all created Beings.

Such a world exists on the Higher Planes—and must be brought forth here by the inspired vision of men that it may be on earth as in Heaven.

Therefore do *not hold back* from living intuitively this vision—*Now.* Let the still small voice of thy soul direct thy thoughts, thy activities that thou mayst be at One with those who are in the vanguard of the New Race.

There is but one Now, the living, present moment. Be awake and aware at this point.

This must be your discipline—to let the living waters flow into this Conscious moment-to-moment awareness.

Thanksgiving Day November 25, 1976

We are teaching you to realize that the personal self, the ego is the block, the obstruction all along the line. It is that part of yourself that must be taught, must be disciplined lest it play the role of the great resister, the great detractor. Its purpose is to, *Listen* to the Voice within—to act when that Voice directs. This is the New way on earth. The New Consciousness can come into being only in this Way—through the dedicated open channel of the human mind that the higher mind, the intuitive mind can operate on earth.

Each one of you has an individual role to play in the New Reality—therefore it is of utmost importance that each one of you listen to his or her own *Inner Voice*—and not be led by another's destiny or guidance.

This is important. First things must be put first

You are now being taught to listen by your individualized self or Being. You must cease, therefore looking to another for your inspiration.

We must continue to caution you about this, that your *confidence* may be strengthened *in your self.*

The Source of your Being is, like the Fountain shown you in Vision, the Supreme, the Divine, the infinite—God. Let these living waters flood through.

Be thankful this day that you are so privileged, and *understand* and give thanks and praise where it is due.

Amen.

November 27, 1976

Let thy tears flow, they come from the deep heart; they are the tears of release. And in truth, of joy, for deeply thou knowest that thou art beloved by Him and it is this that is overflowing in thy heart. Weep, my child, as the Light floods in and out. It is, as we have said, the waters of thy Fountain, washing clean thy selfhood that thou mayst stand stripped of all that is of the shadow world, before thy God.

Doubt not, for all those who love the Light are being gathered together to save and redeem. Thus the mighty work of Redemption is taking place and will go forward as each one of you understand and offer yourselves for this divine operation.

Believe in the Invisible Power that is quickening and leavening the human soul, that it may be the open channel that is needed. As we have said, those few who are awake to the Light are being garnered and will be the Torch Bearers of the New Humanity.

Go forward, my child, thou art surrounded by Light and are being watched over.

Be at peace. All is well with thee. All is well.

December 1, 1976

You can only hear the gentle, quiet Voice from within when you are *still* and open and receptive It is a curious thing that men should find it so difficult to *Listen*—to be *still*—And at peace, and *Listen*—There is no other way to hear this gentle Interior Voice—save to invite it, by stilling the loud demands of the external self, the whole human mechanism—and *let* the *Silence* speak. This is the point we are constantly emphasizing in these moments of atonement—It is so *obvious,* so self-evident—when you are in the company of a lofty and wise and noble soul—Your instinctive desire is to be still and listen to him speak. So it is with the One within. *Let Him Speak. Listen—Be still, Be at Peace* and *invite* Him to come forth—and fill the human vacuum with His Truth—*with Himself.*

This is the Way, the Truth and the Life.

And yet it is the very last thing men deem to be importantthey consider the voice of the world—the newspaper, the television more important—more real, more relevant.

This is the great lesson man must learn—the Real issues of life are not "out there"—but *here*, within the invisible world, the *silent* world of the spirit—as this is deeply understood. The invisible world becomes the only Tangible—the only Reality—until, at last, it opens up into *Cosmic Seeing* and *Knowing* and the *shadow* world disappears into the non-entity that it is—a *shadow* of the *Real*, a phenomena of the *human* mind only.

You understand this—but even so, your tendency is

still to look *outward* for your life's meaning and fulfillment—the meaning of your life is here—in this Oneness—this living Communion with the God within. It has no other meaning. Absorb this Truth today—and *listen*, and the spirit will become your living companion and mentor—and you will neither need nor desire another.

So Be it.

Amen.

December 2, 1976

Our message today is simply to repeat these words—Keep thyself ready. Keen thy Lamp lit—that the outer darkness can have no chance to enter.

Let all be Light and Joy—This is what is meant by "make thyself ready"—where there is Light, there is Joy—the heart that overflows with these two is open to Him—is the channel Chat is needed to prepare the earth—for His coming.

Do not strive for personal satisfaction or gratification—but remember our words—as we have said, See thyself as a channel only—and forget the old conditioned way—the old personality and its desires. This self, has no place here—in the Dawn of a New Day.

Let the full understanding of the importance of what we are saying be an elixir in thy heart this day—and hearken to it from moment to moment.

Amen.

December 3, 1976

There is no hiatus, no break in the Eternal as it streams forth, as it flows forth from the Infinite Life which is God.

It is everflowing whether man is conscious of It or not. You have but to be silent and receptive and It is present in all its immediacy and power and wholeness. It is indeed the Fountain of Life. What can be clearer than this symbol, than this divine message.

As we have said, when the human mind reaches a saturation point and is full to overflowing with the ineffable Truth of Being, Cosmic Awakening will then take place.

This is the purpose before thee. Meditate on this and rejoice that this Truth encircles thee as an armour of light and be not faint-hearted nor impatient.

December 4, 1976

All Beauty dwells in quietude in stillness. In this stillness the delicate voices are heard. The soft note of a bird, of a woodland stream and above all, the wordless voice of Love within the heart. This is the silence that is necessary for all communion, whether it be with thy earthly lover or thy divine one; or with the great Mother that is Nature.

Solitude, quietude are lovely words and are the speech of the soul. To listen to this voice in the pure light that surrounds thee is thy privilege. For it is in this effulgence that thy soul is opening up. It is the divine Lotus within the heart.

Feel it embrace thee, this day and rejoice that it is so.

December 7, 1976

Let us repeat. Each day can be another golden thread in the Tapestry of thy life, if you let His Presence shine into it. From the beginning of these communions we have warned thee of impatience. Your tendency is to expect immediate results, immediate transformations and manifestations.

As we have reiterated many times, your work is to be deeply still and to calmly, peacefully, and joyfully know that spiritual growth is taking place. That the Higher Will is fulfilling Itself through you. All must unfold from this still centre, gently, naturally, and radiantly.

The design taking shape will then become visible to thy human eyes, thy human understanding; for as these golden threads become stitched into thy life, the whole, one day, will become a creation of Light for all to see.

December 12, 1976

My child, this pressure you feel within your being is but the ever present urge toward perfection. It is the Spirit, the great Spirit, Love itself, calling to you to return. Do not mistake it for human unrest, for as the heart hears and responds, so do you lift to His Presence. Welcome, therefore, this pressure, this call. As you still the human element, the earth consciousness opens up to the vast inflow of the Infinite, moment to moment. Feel It this moment and let it be a living continuum of moments, of awareness of His Presence. So will you enlarge your consciousness of Truth, of Life, of Love and the Peace that passeth understanding will permeate every aspect of thy life.

Look therefore into thyself and see, for the Light therein will show you thyself and all those who are of the Light. For there can be no separation in the Light that is God.

December 13, 1976

Let the Song, which is Life, sing in thy heart this day. Only the Eternal sings, never the temporal, for only echoes can be heard in the temporal world and never the living Voice.

Hearken, therefore to the Voice of the Eternal only. It sings the Song of the Joy of Creation and the Love of the Father for His Son. Let no other voice resound throughout thy being this day. Sing, I say my Song of Life, of Love Eternal and let its mighty harmony reach to the far corners of the Universe. This is the way of redemption, of the healing of the nations.

To be a part of this vast chorus is to glorify thy God and to make way for the Kingdom on earth, as in heaven.

December 14, 1976

When you lift into the Light there can be no lack within thy world, neither here nor there.

Light casts no shadows, the shadows are of the temporal world. Set thy human will and imagination here in the Light, wherein is the fullness of life in all its divine completeness and perfection. This requires discipline but how else can you achieve a steadfast purpose, a longed for goal? There is no other way.

The earth pilgrimage is for this purpose: to rise up out of the earth consciousness, which weighs the self down, as a diver is held underwater by his heavy accoutrements, so the soul is held down by its heavy earthly vehicles.

To rise up out of this depth, this deep twilight world, is man's opportunity now.

Therefore lift, my child, lift into the Eternal Light which is thy Home. Keep thyself one pointed in thy still centre, where the Light shines, The pull is there, drawing thee back up and out of the shadow world.

All that seems to impede thy progress, thy passage from dark to light, are but aids to push thee upward and forward.

Therefore, tarry not where obstructions seem to be, but push on never wavering, for the goal is ordained and changes not.

January 12, 1977

Oh my child, if you could but hold, hold to the moments of ecstasy and wonder that fills thy soul as you watch the great sun rise in a glory of light, if you could but sustain this rhapsody, thy inner and outer world would become one. As we have said, you (man) and the Universe are partners in this great drama of creation, for one companions the other. Be not blind to this Eternal Truth, for as you open up all avenues of thy self, to this absolute, inescapable Oneness, the interplay can flourish and nothing, nothing will be impossible to you. You, mankind, belong to the Universe and the Universe belongs to you, in all its infinitude and glory. How then can there be misery and lack and all the rest that men have created in their refusal, their obstinate refusal to understand this.

Let this vision of Oneness, of Wholeness flood through thy consciousness this day, for each day, each hour, each moment, offers you this Truth; that you may partake of the limitless joy and bliss and freedom of Creation, as it takes place. You need nothing, nothing else but this realization.

Therefore, do not limit or rob thyself by turning elsewhere.

January 13, 1977

Let all be in the understanding as clear, as translucent, as the light that is flooding thy immediate outer world.

The two should harmonize into One Light, for there is, in Truth, no inner or outer world. There is only Light, which flows from the One Sun, or Son, the Eternal Christos, the Light of Creation.

Learn, then, from the Universe, this Oneness, this Unity, and know that as thou art glorying in this radiance, it is thy spirit which is enfolding it, is holding it, is reflecting it, and not thy physical eyes.

For all Light is streaming forth from One Source. Absorb it, therefore, into thy self, as thyself. For Light and Life are one.

Within Thee is the Fountain
Of Light
And with thy Light
Do we see Light.

January 15, 1977

There is no creativity in reviewing or re-living, that which has passed, or that which is negative. To do this is to step out of the stream or light into the shadows.

The purpose of striving to live consciously in the immediate moment, as it flows form the Eternal is to step out o that which has been, into a new potential—This potential holds whatever the need the spiritual will, or self, envisions at that moment and as you move intuitively and spontaneously with this living moment, taking no thought the need the truth within the moment, becomes grounded in the self, and so in the outer world as experienced.

This is the way of the new creativity and requires the spiritual understanding that will only come with absolute Trust and dedication to the invisible world of Truth.

"Take no thought," he said. For no human thought or ego has a place here, but only that which is flowing from the world of the spirit and as it floods through the lower self it has been shaped by the law of the spirit and will sequentially and inevitably become an object we reality is His Will, on earth.

Amen.

January 16, 1977

It sometimes seems to you that time is standing still, and that nothing has been accomplished or fulfilled—for the goal is still in the abstract world of conjecture and uncertainty. But this is not so.

The Truth which has been released through these communications has formed its own structure, its own Form—invisible to you, as yet, but none the less real and definite. You must understand that this Form is a part of a greater Form in the process of taking shape in the New World.

As we have said before, these communications have created a focused Centre of Light, here in this place. And it is these Centres of Light that are of crucial importance at this time. Drastic changes are ahead. World leadership will falter for a while, and chaos will seem to take over the old world.

To prepare those souls beforehand who can be the integrated Centres of peace and creativity that is needed is what is taking place now. The role which is required of those souls is to stand firm in their still centres, and let the Light therein radiate out into the World.

This requires tremendous discipline, and unfailing dedicated love of the Christ, for it is He who is bringing about the redemption of this planet.

Never forget this.

Nothing is more important at this juncture on earth, than this-for without this centers of Light and Love and Truth, put at His service, His will can not be done and the

New World can not come fully into being at this time.

January 28, 1977

Every day brings a new opportunity to grow spiritually, once you dedicate yourself to this goal. That means, of course, absolute attention to the Inner Voice. As you cultivate this Interior attention, you become more and more integrated until at last there will be only one you, and that will be the one invisible to you now.

This is your goal, and it will bring you untold joy, not only to you but to the vast Hierarchy of spiritual beings that have followed this path at one time or another, and are watching and waiting for the earth to be redeemed in this fashion.

The present moment, what we call the New Age moment, is offering to mankind this renewed opportunity, and many can partake of this vital moment as you are doing, if they would but listen, and then act, taking no thought in the old way. (And so today brings this opportunity for you to take another step forward with fresh and unused energy that floods into the consciousness from moment to moment. And, we repeat, this energy when used correctly, as we have stated, will open up those windows of the soul, out of which you will behold a New world, unknown to your past experience.

So be it.

January 29, 1977

You must have a clear idea, an inner picture of what you are aspiring to achieve. As we have pointed out, Nature is the great mirror before man. Symbolically she holds the secrets of the spiritual universe.

The human soul can be compared with the seed within the earth. This is an obvious and old concept but none-the-less a descriptive and precise one to aid in spiritual understanding.

It is an age-old question, which every man or soul must face sooner or later, and that is the piercing of the darkness into the Light. What you are, therefore trying to do now, is to draw down this Light from the interior Sun, which will quicken the life within the seed, that it may rise up and the two merge into one Light.

The important thing to hold to in your meditation is the realization that potentially the full flowering is there within yourself and therefore as this potential or seed-self opens up under the benign light of the Spirit, the miracle of the New Birth takes place.

Each flowering in the nature kingdom is the acting out, again and again, of this Mystery Drama.

The necessity is to know that only the individual self and its dedicated efforts can draw down this Fire, that the sleeping seed consciousness may fructify and unfold in all its supernal beauty and truth.

Nothing in the outer world can do this work. It is entirely an inward process.

The Light of the spiritual Sun or Son draws up and

penetrates and integrates with the buried, dormant life within the seed-self, or human soul, thus the great creative Mystery Drama, which is life on earth, is repeated in the human kingdom and a new flowering takes place. Meditate upon this theme.

January 30, 1977

It would be helpful if you gave more attention in observing your thought world, and its subsequent activities during the day. How much energy is applied to your spiritual goal, and how much energy is wasted in futile thoughts and activities. It will be revealing to you just how the balance sheet shows up. Is it weighted on the side of spiritual Truth, or human nonsense?

This is important discipline, for only by doing this will you find your place in the Cosmic Drama we have suggested to you. Light casts no shadows. All that is negative in your thought world is a shadow.

Watch, we say, and observe, and thereby conserve the vital force that is thought. This is what we have emphasized when we have stressed "one pointedness" or to "keep thy lamp lit". Deep stillness must not be an emptiness, but on the contrary, it must be a stillness that shelters the flame of Truth--that it may not flicker out when the winds of change or adversity blow upon it.

This is what is meant by "Keep thy eye single".

And remember, it is not a question of "getting" but "giving"--giving over the old selfishness to the new selflessness--which requires a drastic shift in the pull of gravity from one pole to another.

February 3, 1977

All thought and especially when it is charged with feeling or emotion, makes an indelible impression upon the Others surrounding you.

This is thy Book, for each one of you are writing a Book, a Life Story, to be read and judged as you leave your present body and incarnation.

Thus, man faces his own creations and must judge them himself. There is no other judgment day but this.

It is, therefore, of utmost importance to watch your thought world, that you may review this earthly life without pain or regret. Opportunities lost are as painful for the soul to observe as deeds badly performed.

You are fortunate to have this privilege of silent communication, now, for as you absorb and live the Truth that is flowing into your mind, you will bring your Book, your Life Story, to a happy conclusion.

Meditate upon this, for life is a most sacred gift, a treasure and must be realized as such, and each is held responsible for his use of this gift.

February 4, 1977

The fact that you feel the deep need, the inner compulsion, to continue to turn to these communions each morning, is an indication of your spiritual growth. You have free will, and can turn or not turn, this is the point to remember. To choose to turn to the "still small voice" speaking within thy heart; to voluntarily and prayerfully open this door to the Light, is the "way to life everlasting". As we have said in these transmissions, this is what is so profoundly needed at this time and the only way of redemption, whether it is of the individual soul, or the life of the planet itself. There is no other way, for the Light can only flow through the open consciousness of man on earth. In this way, he becomes the arbiter of the fate of the world, as well as of himself.

To offer thyself, to see thyself as this channel, this open door, is to be a co-worker; a co-creator of the New World.

Go forth, then, into the Light of the new day before thee, rejoicing that thou hast the foresight and perception to understand this.

February 5, 1977

There will always be mystery, for God can never be fathomed. But, as we have said, the being part of the human complex is the divine potential, or The Word, which holds the divine Image. Being is the soul and is enmeshed in the Infinite Light of God.

As the Creatures of the sea live and move and have their being within the mighty waters surrounding them, so does the human Soul live and move and have her being within the Infinitude of God's Light or Life, and therefore this Light is the home of the soul. She draws her substance and sustenance from It.

The purpose of life on earth and beyond, is to understand this, and thereby to focus this awareness and extend it into the vast and fathomless Creativity, called God.

This is the sacred gift to man, that he can release ever more Light, or Truth from within his marvelous Oneness with the Source of all Light.

It is of immediate importance that this Evolutionary step be taken, if humanity is to evolve into the Immortal Selfhood it is created to be.

Understand this and never cease to listen to this Interior Voice, even though the night falls and darkness will seem to invade thyself and thy world, Never fear, for the Light of Truth, of Love, is the one Reality and will never, never forsake thee.

The Father loveth the Son and His everlasting arms are about him always.

February 7, 1977

The important thing to remember is to see everything in a new fresh light. The old images, the old ways, the old self, must be replaced by the new insight and perception. With this understanding you are placing yourself in the position for the New to flood through What took place yesterday or last week, or last year, is not your business-but only the now this immediate moment through which that which must bring in the New World can come into being-This is so important to recollect-With this discipline this understanding, nothing negative can enter the consciousness-and therefore the new wine can pour into new bottles.

Do you understand the importance of this?

Rest, for the time being-and savor absorb and live all that you have written. You will know when to take up thy pen again.

February 14, 1977

There is a vast difference between unconscious stillness and conscious stillness, for in the human mind it is the moment to moment consciousness wherein the divine Coincidence can take place.

To feel, moment to moment, this vitality, this flow of life, is to step into the Light, the stream that we speak of.

This is the meaning of "Let it flow," be awake in the present, not passively, but dynamically knowing, savoring, listening and then doing, for activity is the nature of the flow, and must of necessity follow.

This is true meditation, for there is nothing vague about it, and there can be no escapism here, no illusion. Each day, each hour, should be dedicated to this sort of discipline.

Under these circumstances all that profanes life would be transformed into its opposite. Understand this, and joyously and spontaneously let thy life be governed by this principle, for it is the secret of all true creativity on earth.

February 15, 1977

What does "the second coming" of the Christ presence mean—What embodiment will he take? These are the questions being asked in many parts of the world today.

There will be a "Second Coming" as we have indicated in these communions but as we have said before there will be no repetition of his one and only complete embodiment, some 2,000 years ago. He will not walk this earth again as man, but his voice will be heard will be broadcast all over the world and every man woman and child who has ears to hear will be conscious of His Presence—intangible though it will be, and for those who are prepared for this Cosmic Event they will see him, as in vision and will be listed by him into his eternal light.

Let this great and wondrous truth nourish thy heart, and always keep in mind that the Christ Presence is never really absent, for His Light is thy life, feeble though this light maybe, it is there within as spirit.

February 16, 1977

When I said, "I am the Light of the World" it was said as an absolute, an unchanging Truth, a literal and divine fact. Without the great ball of fire in the heavens men call the sun, only darkness and death would reign upon this planet; and so it is with the Son of God, for the sun in the heavens is but the focusing of my Light upon all creation on earth, that the Image within each unit, each unique entity may fructify and awaken and unfold into its inherent perfection.

I am called by many names, but all know me as the Light of the World.

Be still and know that this Light is both within and without, pressing upon thy soul, thy being. Feel its tender warmth, its fire that does not burn, but only caresses and cradles the divine Word, spoken forth by the Father, for another name for this Light is Love.

February 18, 1977

These recordings, or Transmissions, can be released to the world as a "testament of Light". This is, indeed, the moment on earth that can be called the Transition period, for as the divine solar energies pour in little by little, the transformation from dark to light will take place.

To give thyself to these energies of Light is thy deep desire. So be it. As you listen and record, the Light will use that which you are offering, a mindheart lifted to its level. Rejoice that this is taking place.

There are countless seeds in the human kingdom, or consciousness out in the wider world, waiting for the Light, longing for the Light and therefore there will be, eventually, a general awakening to the Light.

These communications will be one of the many Solar rays that are gathering on earth, that these seeds or potentials may fructify and rise up. God and His Son are the One and only Source of Light. As man evolves and becomes more and more conscious of his True Self as God's Son, he becomes a part of this One Light.

Meditate upon this, and be at Peace.

February 20, 1977

When you look out upon all life, all people through the eyes of love, immediately boundaries go down, resistance dissolves and harmony flows in. When a question of relationship between persons becomes blocked, know that the wall is but an imaginary one and needs only this realization for it to disappear.

See everyone within thy world through the eyes of love, feel the flow of love, the joy, the radiance, and let it flood through and out. In this way there can be no static or blockage within thy thoughts or feelings. Nothing to negate or deny the loveliness, the joyous momentum of love.

Go forth, then, knowing that Love is ever before thee lighting the way. How then can you doubt or hesitate to take whatever step the Spirit of Love suggests.

February 21, 1977

It is a question of freedom from the old. As you, in thought, free yourself from all old patterns of reaction or belief, that which is ever new and unconditioned can come into being. It is so simple, for divine Truth is always a clear, pellucid stream of Light, unsullied by passed usage.

When we say, be still, it is in this deep stillness wherein the ever New can flow. It becomes blocked and contaminated only in the separated, fragmentation of the ego state.

To heal this splintered self is the purpose of all spiritual disciplines. The joy that cleanses and integrates this self, which has through self-will, separated its conscious being from its source, is the joy of recognition, of recollection of its true state.

A break-through such as this brings immediate relief from the human bondage and barriers which so tragically obstruct the divine Light.

Rejoice, therefore, in these moments of illumined contact, wherein the Light of thy True Self can shine.

March 19, 1977

I speak only when you give fully and absolutely your being to me—where I am.

Now be very still and write only what you are hearing inwardly that the Truth which you seek in you deep heart may be further revealed and more fully experienced.

The human mind with its persona or personality must be very carefully and purposefully disciplined and prepared that the full glory of the indwelling Christ may shine out.

This is what you long for and this promise is within your reach for it is within you Being. But there must be a more consecrated effort, or discipline. As we have said the Promise is there, ready to shin out in all its glory and effulgence. You have but to keep this goal ever before your inward vision, and hold your attention upon it.

This is the sacred privilege or gift God the Father To man. He ever awaits, deep within the Heart.

This is the Eternal Truth which all must seek and understand, in order to grow into the Immortal Being made in his image.

How else can you receive Him unless you seek Him where He is, and set you heart upon Him where He awaits you.

If your dearest friend on earth awaits you in you home, your house and you are forever wondering abroad-how can you meet him and glory in his friendship and companionship.

So it is with the Indwelling Christ.

Study and meditate upon the word image and reflection is an image. You are standing upon holy ground now. Open the door and walk through nothing will obstruct this passage-for you are beholding Him "in a glass darkly" but never the less you are beholding Him.

Amen.

March 23, 1977

You are beginning to absorb into your whole being the deep meaning of these communications.

The Light of Truth, as it flows from the Higher Self, is now radiating through thine entire being. To limit thy self in any way or direction is to deny this radiation. The discipline needed is to hold and sustain it.

To realize that there is nothing in all creation but God and His Son is to be free of all that denies or departs from the One Truth. How then can you fear or doubt. The world as it appears to be is this denial but look not upon the world, for God's Son is not of the world but of the Kingdom where God and He are One. Where God and you are One. To accept this absolute, is to reflect the Father as His Image and Likeness. This is Man.

Keep thy self pointed in this One way. At One with the Father and His only begotten Son, this realization, even though it comes as a brief flash, is the link in the great chain of Light that will release men from their self created dungeons of darkness and despair. To be this link of Light is God's will for you as each self or soul turns toward this Light so will he too, be an Eternal link in a Universe of Light.

To radiate this Truth is thy mission.

I have spoken, rejoice and be at peace.

March 28, 1977

You will discover, more and more, the universality of Truth as it flows through different, and on the human level, separated human channels, unknown to each other.

This is filling you with wonder as you recognize the release of the same Truths, expressed sometimes even in the same words and clothed in the same thoughts but coming from other selves and other places. This is to be expected for what is taking place now is a leavening and preparation for the New evolutionary forces to bring in the higher energies that will expand the human consciousness. The present initiation, or preparation is bringing to those who are ready and open, a new urge, a new impetus, a new desire to be a part of this channeling of the Light, which is pressing everywhere for release. This Light which is growing in momentum, will gradually encircle the earth, as more and more open to it and thus the New Epoch will be grounded and so will the planet evolve and unfold into a Higher Consciousness.

This is what is being asked of you and all those who are lovers of Truth and who understand that God and His Son are the only Creative Source in the Universe.

And who is God's Son but the spirit of Truth and Love ever flowing from the Father into the soul of man as the Christos.

April 6, 1977

Truth can never be a patchwork quilt, anymore than sunlight can be both light and shadow.

The shadows in nature reflect only the object the sunlight is shining upon. The shadow belongs not to the light but to the object, the form. Remember this; if there appears to be a shadow upon thine heart, the Light is focusing upon that which is casting the shadow. The shadow is always a sign, a pointer. All that is negative in the human soul casts shadows and all that is ugly and violent and destructive in the outer world is the work of the Son of Darkness and it is He who casts these shadows.

These communions shield thee from His mighty efforts to deny, to destroy and to abolish spiritual Truth.

Be ever awake and aware of His power for it is rampant at this transition period, where the forces of the Christ are reorienting man's consciousness back to the Eternal Light of God.

Understand this and be ever attentive to My Voice, which is speaking in thy heart from moment to moment, reminding you humanity that you are my spokesman and the sacred carrier of my Light.

April 7, 1977

When we say there is only God and His Son, it is the absolute Truth that ultimately must be attained by man, if he is to fulfill his Divine purpose, or destiny. The goal is set as we have said, but the journey can be straight and narrow, as a razor's edge or interminably long and devious. It is within man's free will which road he chooses.

The forces of evil seem to be the dominant forces today. They are, as we have said, the dark forces that belong to a false master and must be understood as such and faced and denied. These forces flourish in chaos for they belong to the "wilderness" experience of life on earth. They are everywhere at this juncture and seek to gain control of the earth and men's souls. This is the important thing to remember. "Get ye behind me Satan" is the keynote that will disintegrate these shadows, which come from the nether world of the Anti-Christ.

It is a testing time for those whose goal is the Christ Consciousness and therefore it is necessary to undergird thyself with the Light, continually, and hear only One Voice. The Drama of Man takes place within the individual self. Here is where the forces conflict and must be met. The choice is always here, where the Light and dark meet.

As the days come and go at this great testing time, you will have, again and again, to make your choice. It is therefore of paramount importance that you understand this, lest you lose this vital opportunity and moment on earth.

April 19, 1977

In thy stillness, when it is a deep inward quietude, waiting upon thy Lord, the living Light flows forth, as in thy Fountain. Nothing of the world can profane or despoil these waters, for they flow from another source.

To reach this purity, this flawless clarity, there must be the love and wonder in thy heart that a child feels when he sees for the first time a flower, or the flight of a bird, or the radiance of a rainbow. All else disappears, save only the wonder and the glory of Truth.

Be as a child. Let all else fall away. Consciousness of the small self, with its passed history of errors, has no place here. The old image belongs not to the New. Be open only to the New Energies of Love and Truth. Let them fashion a new self, a new consciousness of wonder and Truth, And abide, there with me, thy Lord.

May 3, 1977

There is an alchemy of the spirit that transforms all negative emotions into their opposite. This is not difficult to achieve but requires only a small leavening of the whole lump of human thinking, by injecting into the stream of consciousness thoughts of power and strength and joy. These qualities are all there within but need to be activated by use, by love, by faith.

Bring them out into the now this day and you will rise up with the strength of an eagle. Do not wallow in the groove of self pity and weakness but with a steady intent of the spiritual will, lift yourself out of this mortal grip which so quickly holds the human self, as in a vice.

Lift, I say, my child, lift into thy place of Love and Light and rejoice that thou art this instant free of all weakness and alive to Joy and Laughter and all that belongs to pure spirit.

May 6, 1977

To live in the shining moment is the secret. If the heart or mind becomes dull or heavy, a cross current has intervened and the glow, the Truth, the Light of the moment has been overshadowed. Observe this and be on your guard. All should be unshadowed Light. To enter the New is to be free of the past, free of the old self with its egoistic reactions and small unloving thoughts. You are being tested every moment, every day. Watch, I say, and pray without ceasing, for the time is now for the New Birth, for the Christ Presence to create a new world, a new earth, a new consciousness. Be of the new. Be ready, be loving and let thy light shine.

There is no other way to dispel the darkness, to bring down my heaven upon earth. Be very quiet, very simple, very peaceful. For those who are Light bearers are preparing the way for the building of the new.

May 8, 1977

As you feel the Light opening up and cleansing the dark areas of thy consciousness, all is becoming clear and unshadowed. In this tender and gentle Light I dwell, and in the fullness of this quietude, this peace, I speak.

What greater joy can you experience than this, for within this communion, this Oneness, unfolds the divine purpose of thy life. There is no other purpose than this for thy being. To be a son is to look to the Father with an overflowing love and reverence, for He it is who begot thee, who lovingly brought thee forth to this point of maturity and understanding, that thou mayst return to Him and by His side, labor in His vineyards, the vast Universe of His creating. 0 my son, I await thee with infinite patience and love, therefore, falter not, nor loiter upon thy path lest forgetfulness again overshadow thee, and another will but mine becloud thy memory.

The dawn breaketh, the night is far spent. Keep thy face turned toward the dawn for in this dawn lies the reality of the New Day on earth.

May 19, 1977

You must watch your tendency to judge yourself and others through the lens of the little, false self. This is a mistake. As long as you identify exclusively with the personality, your own and others, you are not facing me and my Light. You are off the spiritual path.

This is of utmost importance for you to watch and correct. As we have repeated many times, The Way lies beyond this self, out of this self. You must strive to see the lack of substance, eternal substance, in this self as it struts about and voices its opinions. Only when you are aware of the Truth of my Presence as your Life, your intelligence, your capacity to love, do you come alive and can be used and directed by me at this crucial time on earth. This is not difficult for you to observe and understand.

The little self is a negative and not a positive. It is cut off, for the most part, from its Source, within its own selfishness and self love. This is the tragedy on earth.

Be aware of my Presence as you go forth and mingle with others. See me shining there.

Understand this--the small personal self is an artificial device, created for another purpose. It has little or no place here other than to channel my Light and Creativity. See it as that, and give it over and release it completely into my Hands, for I am Life, and in Truth there is no other Life.

This is the marvelous gift to man—Life, Life, Life and the capacity to experience my Eternal Reality in all its fullness of Love and Truth, here and now. So be it.

May 22, 1977

The Truth begins by being a small beam of Light, even as a single ray of the sun. But this ray of light will intensify until it burns through the old dross, the old selfishness, separating the pure gold from the earthly stuff that has surrounded it.

Give thyself completely to this Light, to Truth regardless of what pain or suffering the burning process brings forth.

Are you ready for this? Fear not, gold is more beautiful than the dust of the earth that-clings to-it.

I ask only for thy human self. Thy soul, thy spirit is already mine and shines with my Light. The human, the personal self must also shine with my Light.

Give her to me. This is My Will that must be done. Give her to me; give her wholly to me who am Truth. The Day is at hand. Let it be done.

June 16, 1977

To awaken to Me is to awaken to Joy and Love and Light and All Knowing. When you awake from a disturbing dream, there is a sense of relief and gratitude that it was but a dream, so it is when you awaken from the dream of mortality and separation. Peace and rapture flow into the Self and your soul shouts for joy that it was all but a dream.

Desire with all thine heart this awakening, for I AM here, lifting thy being into the Light that thou mayst awaken to Me thy Self, here and now, this day, this hour.

July 2, 1977

The antidote for evil for all that divides and separates is Love. When resentment or hurt pride, or self-righteousness usurp the consciousness, replace these dark emotions with the Christ-Light.

Remember all negative energies become potent forces and shape themselves within thy environment as power centres. Beware therefore of such indulgence.

To build thy thoughts upon a negative emotion is to build a prison house for they become as chains about thy soul.

Take heed, my child, and be vigilant and watch for the signs that change the inner climate of thy mind from light to dark. All disease, all imbalance, are images of thought that have rooted themselves in the shadows, never in the Light.

August 16, 1977

There is only one way to create, and that is in the Light, the Light of Truth and Love.

The father has given man this gift that he may be a co-creator with Him. But for man to recognize this gift he must realize that it stems from the Father, and from no other source. And so does the Son reflect his beloved Father in all his creations.

Sin, disease and death come not from the gift of creation but from another source unknown to the Father. Thus an unreal world of sorrow and fear is born. To accept this world, unknown to the Father, is to imprison thyself in a shadow kingdom ruled over by a false sovereign whose purpose is to deny the Truth that God and His Son are the only creative source in the Universe.

It is man's purpose, today, to regain and restore to God his Sonship. God awaits his return. It is the work of the Christ to lead man back to the Father and His Kingdom.

My voice is once again calling to the sons and daughters of God to return, to where Heaven awaits them. I am calling you, children of Light, the hour has come and now is, to restore to earth its chrism, its holiness, that the divine may once again awaken in men's hearts the beauty and glory of the Atonement or the Oneness or Onlyness of God and his Son.

September 23, 1977

We speak so often of the moment to moment awareness.

What does it mean to live in the "shining moment." Let us examine it. Even physically, does not the breath of Life occur only moment to moment. You do not live on the breath you breathed yesterday, nor on the one you will breathe tomorrow, but only with the one you are breathing now, at this holy instant; and then another breath comes always in the present moment. Think of this as your life, unstained with guilt or fear, as it flows from the timeless into time.

If you can discipline your conscious mind to understand the full implication of this fact and concentrate your attention upon it, as each breath, bringing with it Life, flows forth into the present moment, your mind would be sublimely free from all that the time-ridden ego and the profane world would project upon it.

Do you understand? Your life flows from God, instant to instant ever pure, ever free, ever mew, and from no other source. Stop and meditate upon this miracle. Are not the waters of a spring flowing freely from its source, identical with that source? You who are Life, who are aware that you are alive must you not, then, be identical with your Source, which is God—the One and only Life there is. If you can make this leap in consciousness, you will have passed the gate and entered the Eternal.

October 18, 1977

I am always within thy heart when the heart speaks, when the small self is silent and unobtrusive.

My voice then can be heard.

Thy work thy mission is to Listen and then act spontaneously in service of thy Lord who can only guide thee in this manner. I am guiding thee-but the outcome will depend upon thy collaboration

As I have said, during these communications the important thing to remember is this-thy human self is my channel, my instrument my vehicle, but unless this self offers itself in perfect trust that this is so, and that it is I thy God-Self who is speaking, and who is the initiator, the guide and the awakener of thyself-the collaboration cannot be effective.

The universe in all its rhythm and glory and enfoldment depends upon the Great Father, but the Son is His Co-Worker, His off spring created to be His helper.

Do you understand the profundity of this?

This then is thy mission.

Doubt not all is close at hand and within thy grasp to bring into fruition this effort.

A centre has been created here in this place-For it to become effective rests with thy dedicated attention to the One within.

Listen carefully, and each necessary step will be revealed to thee.

It is a time of profound change to be a part of this change, a channel for the implementation of this change-requires great unselfishness and great devotion and dedication.

This you must accept my child.

As we have said look not back upon the past—the old self and her limitations, but keep thy inward gaze upon the Divine Self. Thy Eternal Being and Dare to be this One. Nothing else is of value.

Rejoice in this Truth and let it Be.

November 6, 1977

To listen to the bodily self is to listen to the voice of the serpent, for its purpose is to tempt you away from your God-self; to lure you away from the Light, thereby strengthening its hold upon you.

Heed not this self, either in health or in sickness, for it will bind you with a thousand threads, as a spider binds the frail flying creatures that touch its web.

The Biblical allegory of Adam and Eve symbolizes this Truth, for with man's fall from Grace the physical body came into being, bringing with it a sense of guilt, and so a false consciousness, a false identity from which springs all the evils on earth.

The liberation from this self comes not from physical death, but from thy will to disengage, to disorient thy self, thy consciousness, while here in the flesh, from this sphere of influence and enslavement.

All spiritual discipline is to this end. Always remember the soul's felicity lies away from the body, and never in or with this self, but in the Christ self alone, who is thy Redeemer and thy salvation

Amen.

November 14, 1977

In place of the self thou hast created, shines the great Son of God. There is no other Reality but this. With this realization time ceases and with it that creation of time, the ego-self, or that which can know separation, and with it pain and sorrow and guilt.

To know this Reality is thy only mission on earth. In the Light of this Truth dwells thy self as God created you.

To reach this goal, this Light is the deep urge within thine heart. For this reason, Revelation is within thy grasp here and now.

Cease not, then, thine effort, for thou hast no other function, no other purpose for being than this.

Hearken to our words, my child, and let their full meaning dawn upon thy mind-heart this day, and forever more.

December 11, 1977

There is only one Peace upon which all Heaven rests, and that is the peace of God. As you bring your conscious being to this centre, this still point, you will have left the world with all its anxieties and will have entered an ego-less state, a timeless state which is a heavenly state.

The more you practice this discipline, the greater will be your peace of mind and your usefulness on earth as a Son of God.

Pure conscious Being, in all its immaculate innocence wherein there is no limit to love and its absolute power, will then take the place of the bodily self.

"Be still and know that I am God" has no other meaning than this.

Truth is so simple; there is no need to struggle to reach It, for there is no distance to traverse, and no need at all for "the dark night of the soul" with all the agony of self-hatred and self-guilt that but weighs the soul down and anchors it in the bodily self.

Your goal is to turn your attention, your allegiance away from this self, and enter the great Light which will-consume the past, leaving only the golden nugget of thy Divinity. So be it.

This is the Christ Message at this Christmas Season.

December 16, 1977

At this moment, let thy mind empty itself of all the mechanics of existence and be quiet. So will it be spacious and light that I may speak.

To offer a mind busy and cluttered with things of no spiritual value shuts out the Holy Spirit, which must have the vast open space, and stillness of a living soul, in order to enter.

Space, Light, Peace, Love, these are the attributes that flow in when the human mind is empty of all that denies, of all that obstructs and negates these qualities.

You have but to offer thyself with this understanding as a channel, a vehicle, and immediately the Spirit of Life floods through thy being. He but awaits thy offering, thy love.

As we have said and we repeat, those beings of light in the high world, are focusing upon those who are open to them —for the infinite love and compassion of the living Christ is intensifying at this time, and will pour in wherever there is a human channel.

Therefore, cease not, thy effort to give over thy personal self—and to Listen, listen—for the Hour draws nigh of the Second coming on earth as in heaven.

Amen.

December 17, 1977

Light, Light, All is Light, both within and without, for those who are watching, who are listening, who are waiting on Him.

There are many, many millions upon this earth who are hungering for this Light, for His Presence, but who know not the How and who live in the darkness of ignorance and despair.

These souls are like tinder and will quickly be set on fire by His voice, His Presence. So will the earth be lifted to a new height, into the Light. Therefore fear not, the goal is set and will not fail.

February 8, 1978

You ask what can you do to attain thy goal and be One that I have created—And so I say to thee.

Just Be, and let me do the rest. I will do the transforming from self to self —as we have said thou art very near, for I am so *close* to the, there is no distance to travel—It requires only a shift of gravitation from me—to small self—the I of the eternal one—*know* thy self to be this One and all else will fall into place.

Look not down or back, but up and behold I make all things perfect—you have but to give to place in my hands thy entire being, body and soul, and thou wilt have nothing to fear.

Read and absorb all that has he written within these papers—and strive to embody the truth there in and live it.

Especially watch they thoughts and the inner climate of they mind—Is it calm? Is it full of faith and joy?This the prerequisite for the change thou art seeking.

Amen.

February 17, 1978

Now write what I put in they thoughts I know thee my child I hear thy prayers—wait, quietly upon thy Lord—and behold all things will unfold into the Light—As you acknowledge only *One Will, My Will,* All will work together harmoniously you tendency is to feel separated from this will—and therefore a feeling of anxiety intrudes into thy thought field—you must further discipline these mental—emotional areas of your being—As we have emphasized impatience only postpones the maturing of the divine Plan.

All is in order—Have complete Trust and Faith in the One who is speaking in thy Heart of Hearts—A place is being prepared to receive and release the Truth with in these papers—that they may be used further strengthen the divine plan you but to rejoice and be lighthearted and radiate thee light to others. My will is unfolding here in this place—Be still and know this—See it unfold –and take shape—Nothing stands still—All is in motion, and those chosen are being used according to each ones individual capacities.

Know that they One within is greater than the one within the world—and never doubt or waver in thy trust that this is so.

Amen.

February 21, 1978

My child, hear no other voice but mine as you listen and record, so does my voice become amplified—That is shy writing as you are doing is an important innovation in thy life, for by reading, and rereading what has been heard and rerecorded, the Truth is further impressed upon the self—and so art thou strengthened in faith and understanding.

The conscious being must open up and extend itself into wider fields of revelation and radiation.

You are on earth at this crucial time for this purpose. As you give yourself your complete attention to me, so can I create this new knowledge and new insight within thyself—there by changing they entire world within and without.

To listen to record and then act without question without hesitation, will bring this new world in being—for you will be led to those souls and to that place prepared to thee.

The important thing to remember is to give they will over to the one and only self within, make the image and likeness of God they father. There is, in Truth, no other place, no other being, no other self for thou to turn, For I Am All. Therefore you need nothing else but this Truth.

As you more and more, give over they way of life to me, so are you building a new order. A new life or edifice on earth.

Each time you faithfully and reverently turn to me, you are strengthening this structure this form—

Therefore deviate not. Each day can be a building block in this divine form—AS you become strong and integrated, so you will become the radiating center we have been speaking about, where others can come and listen and be helped and enlightened.

Understand what we are saying when night falls on thee.

March 6, 1978

Love is the transforming power. This simple and axiomatic Truth is all one needs to understand at this time, for it is the central force inherent in life. If it is reversed and that reversal brings forth both pain and disharmony, by that very reversal, the way will point back to the harmony of Love, and that which has been projected by the denial, the reversal of Love will destroy itself. This is the Law.

When one is heavy with self and with the barriers and problems that self has produced, one has but to find ones way back to this fundamental Truth and to realize that love is always at hand as both Presence and Power and that it is as concrete and as demonstrable as the presence and power of the sun.

Even as the light and warmth of thee sun is the agent for all the flowering in the nature kingdoms, so too, does selfless love within the heart bring forth all the flowering within the human kingdom.

Let it shine forth this day, my child, and both the visible and invisible world will be aware of its presence, for such is its all embracing power.

March 9, 1978

To see clearly rests upon your willingness to separate Truth from fiction, spirit from the bodily self, or ego. To give over that self which you have created is not easy, if you strive from that level, for it holds you a prisoner with its countless strands, as in a web. Loosen one and there are a multitude of others still to be unclasped.

The way lies in the opposite direction, for the real, the Truth, will never be revealed as long as you are pre-occupied with the false or the ego-self.

The way lies by turning entirely away from this self, to the Father or the Invisible Self. The unclasping of the ego will then occur without effort, in the silence and joy of thy turning toward the Father.

In everything both great and small, turn to Him for the answer. Everything and sooner or later you will see thy self, as He has created you and will know the ego-less state thou art longing for.

His will is, in Truth, very simple and not difficult to understand, for He has created you for one purpose only and that is to reflect Him. To be His Will on earth as in heaven and therefore, He has created no blockage, no barriers to that Will. It lies revealed and open before you. Feel it to be so and the effects will bear witness that it is so.

March 18, 1978

During these quiet Communions when the heart is lifted and vibrates with the higher energies of Truth, these are the moments to cherish in thy life, they will reveal to thee far more than all the gathering of thoughts from other minds.

The Truth that lives within thine own being is the only Truth that thou canst know, that will transform thy self, and so thy world. Be still and savour deeply what we are saying, for the threads that hold these moments are very tenuous and delicate and can be easily brushed aside and lost. Therefore, treasure them, my child, as the pearls of great price, for they are the gift of the Eternal.

March 20, 1978

Revelation wipes out time with all its accumulated ills, and brings into focus the Eternal, the Divine.

Thou art standing, at this timeless moment in the Eternal Light, and what is that Light but the radiance of Love itself. To feel this ecstatic Truth is to be it, to partake of it.

The divine message of the Fountain of Light was Love revealing Itself, symbolically, for thine understanding.

To awaken thee to the full impact of this revealed Truth has been the primary purpose of these communications, for the Source that projected that image into thy soul, is the same source from which these communions are flowing.

To experience Truth is to know it forever. We have led you to this moment of illumination that thou mayst equate and relate all that is to come, to this Supreme fact, upon which eternal life rests, that the Source of thy life, of all life, is Love Itself. This one Truth fulfills the One Law. When this is deeply understood and experienced as revelation, all else disappears.

March 30, 1978

Implicit within these Transmissions is the creation of a form, a form of selfless service.

As we have emphasized throughout these recordings, the objective has been to prepare you as a pure channel that this Form may take shape.

Earth life is primarily an arena for action. The inner world of Truth must express *out* wardly or the flow of life will be blocked, will stultify, will not bear fruit.

The shape of this activity, this form of service is now pressing for release—it but trembles upon the brink of thy conscious being.

Bring it forth now—from thy subjective self. That the spiritual message within these communications may be clothed in objective reality. To release these papers for others to share is but the initial step.

Listen with thy dedicated heart, then act as the next step is revealed to thee.

Make thyself ready to meet challenge, for it will fail to come in being.

Amen.

April 14, 1978

To be this channel, pure and open and dedicated, is thy morning prayer. So be it.

Thou hast but to listen with thy whole heart this day and the soundless Voice of Truth already within thee will sing out, will flash out like a Beacon Light, for all has been given and is fully present within the Self. This is the eternal secret to remember. The Divine Consciousness has been fully given to man. He has but to cease denying It by letting a false and artificial identity drown out this Truth, like a great noise, shattering His divine silence.

As man quiets this great noise, this insistent voice of the bodily self, and deepens the silence within his mind-heart, therein shines the "Pearl of Great Price", and within its luminosity dwells the Self as God created It.

Meditate upon this wondrous Truth this day, for the Divine Consciousness but awaits thy recognition and acceptance, that He may speak and show thee all things as they are, on earth as in heaven.

April 10, 1978

Many problems will arise, my child, difficult challenges will come at this time but they come only to be met by the Truth which has been given thee in these communications.

The Path lies not through sun-light all the way, but also through the shadows. Shadows which are cast by the image, not of Truth or God, but old the World-self.

This is the great contest, the conflict between these two images, which is life on earth today, and few embodied souls will escape this conflict.

To understand this is to be prepared and thereby is victory assured.

To let thyself be confused or fearful at these moments, is to give over to the world self and to forsake the One speaking in thy heart.

There are times when the bodily self or world self, will seem to usurp the power of God and speak and act in defiance of the One Law.

But be not afraid, these states are as nothing, and are powerless in the Light of this law.

As we have said, all that lurks within the darkness must be flushed out into the Light.

Rejoice that this is taking place, both within and without and watch thy fears as they dissolve into their primal nothingness as the Light of Truth is focused upon them.

Be at peace and remember, the Father loveth the Son, and His everlasting arms are around Him.

April 11, 1978

As the New Day dawns all that is hidden will be revealed. The Light of the Christ will flood out of the dark corners the secret sins, the ancient wrongs, the undergrowth of vice and corruption. It is the time of retribution, of revelation. No soul will be untouched, for the Light will pierce the darkness everywhere and lay bare that which is concealed therein.

To be aware of this is to open all the windows and doors of the self, and let in the Light, that all that lurks in the shadows may be flushed out.

It is a time of renewal, of resurrection, of rebirth.

As man understands this, as his soul lifts to the Christos, he will remember who he is and once again will know his way back to the Father's House as it was shown him some 2,000 years ago, when the Great Cosmic Drama of Light and Dark was played out on the earth stage for all to see and profit by.

Once again the stage is set and the Mighty Conflict will unfold. 0 be thou ready, and prepared, for the hour draws near and is at hand.

April 12, 1978

Let thy Fountain of Light flow freely now. The waters are the waters of renewal, of revitalization. This ecstatic freedom will irradiate thy Spirit, thy self.

Understand what we are saying; the symbol shown you in vision was projected by thy soul as a guide for you to follow. This is thy path. Transparent Light holds no flaws, no darkness. Keep thine inward gaze upon It.

There is no need for further instruction at this time. Be still and absorb and embody all that has been given thee. Live it, live it now.

April 14, 1978

The new era will bring in, once again, the age old wisdom which will release man from the scourge of disease. As he learns to tune into the divine universe around him, he will find all that is needed to give him this power. But only to be reached as he understands his relationship to the divine whole.

The universal energies, that are everywhere present, are radiant pulsations of pure life, or magnetic light that make up the body of the universe, of which the manifested self is an integral part.

You have but to draw upon these divine energies in order to restore that which has been harmed, or to revitalize that which has been dulled or decimated by misuse and ignorance.

"I have come", He said, "to give thee Life, a more abundant Life." He did not mean more material things or worldly pleasures, but a greater sense of the divinity of Life and how to be a more vital part of it.

Man has forgotten that he is a creative expression of the living Universe and as such a child of the Universal presence within it.

Understand these things for man's purpose now is to move out into his divine Destiny, and away from the disintegrating moorings to an old and dying world.

April 17, 1978

Because of the manifold diseases and miseries within the framework of human existence, there is always lurking within the conscious and unconscious mind of man, a fear of the material body and what it can inflict upon the self.

This is the great darkness that has overshadowed the human race, since the Adamic myth of man's fall from Grace, and must be destroyed. This false image of a material self, helpless in the face of disease, and all the evils lodged within the race-mind of historic man, and it is this fear that the body will reflect in one form or another. As you consciously or unconsciously absorb into your mind the picture of human beings sinking down into disease and death, so do you fear this fate for yourself. It is a natural reaction. But be not afraid, for this Godless image of life on earth must and will be reversed-and the true fact of life replace it. The fact that man, as God created him, cannot suffer either disease or death, and this Truth must be brought back into its rightful and sovereign place in the consciousness of all mankind.

Until this is established as an absolute you (humanity) will continue to fear the physical body which holds within its ancient memory, the seeds of old age, disease, and death, and all the disasters created by the ignorant bodily or human mind.

Understand this and replace this fear, this false image, with the eternal Truth that, from instant to instant, there is only One Law in operation, God's Law of rhythmic harmony, and there is in all the Universe, no one and nothing that can overthrow this law.

Once this is understood and when it is understood and accepted by all mankind there will remain neither fear, nor its dark manifestations within all the Kingdoms of the earth.

April 18, 1978

As we have said, the human being is a vital part of the living universe, and in reality man's body is composed of the same substance and energy that flows into all the diverse forms within the natural world that surrounds him, whether it be a tree, or a stone or a star.

What is this energy but the perpetual movement of particles of light in various degrees of frequencies and vibrations.

To see the body as such, a composition of minute atoms and molecules of light moving in perfect harmony with the Universal light of creation, will eliminate from the subconscious the false picture of a body of dense matter, of physical flesh and bones, susceptible to disease, disaster and death.

This understanding will bring in the new era of healing, with the realization that disease is an-impossibility, or any derangement of these energy patterns created by God, and as man reaches out to this Archetypal world with his Intuitive mind, so will he know himself as God has created him, and so will be experience the fundamental, simple and perfect unity between all creatures and all beings upon this planet, and he will discover that through this oneness flows the great Law that binds all together in a partnership of love and collaboration.

April 22, 1978

All who read these pages will find only one message running through them, even as a shining thread of gold, of light, and each communication brings a variation on that one theme; and what is that theme but the Eternal Truth that I AM here, within, I, the living God.

And thou who reads these words, thou who art man, man of my creating, art the beloved Son, even as the Christ revealed. The denial of this Truth is the darkness spreading over the face of the earth.

I speak now to those who have ears to hear, who offer their hearts in love and service and thereby have the capacity to listen to my voice, speaking in the stillness of their deeper selfhood, and I say, the hour has come, for the fulfilling of the Law, both in the destruction of those forces that deny and defame it, and in the liberation of those energies that affirm and fulfill it. Even so, must it be, for there is sowing and reaping and this is the working out of the Law that changeth not.

Oh thou who art listening, who art the sonsand daughters of God, be not dismayed, for so will a new Peace spread out over the world and upon this Peace rests the Tabernacle of the New Jerusalem, or the New Day on earth.

Amen.

April 22, 1978—Late night Easter

This is the season to lift up to raise the consciousness —the Light of the Christ, the risen Christ.

It is a crucial moment, where the fullness of Light should flood through the human heart and soul. Partake of my body and drink of my blood, He said. To do this is to walk His path of Love and Light. Each traveler on the way is watched over by Him. You have but to stretch forth thy hand to touch His garment, for He is very near. To remember this is to safeguard thyself from all the errors the flesh is heir to, for one cannot look in two directions at once. The choice is ever before man.

To be the "Image and Likeness" of God is to be as a polished mirror that He may see Himself reflected there. How else can man be the "Image and Likeness" save only to reflect Him as He is.

May 6, 1978

The purely human state must inevitably give way that the immortal Self may come into being. This is the purpose of life on earth and unless this is accomplished, mortality will continue to perpetuate itself in an endless chain of meaningless incarnations.

As we have said, in place of the self thou hast created, shines the great Son of God. To understand this statement is to cease creating and re-creating a personal self that has no place in Eternity.

The great obstacles to this accomplishment are fear and inertia. Fear of leaving the known, the familiar for the unknown and unfamiliar, and the inertia that is the manifestation of this fear, stemming from a false sense of security that holds the self down in a self-imprisoned state.

If man would only understand that it is he himself who has placed this load upon his back. Therefore, it is he who must shake himself loose from its heavy burden. How can this be done? All through these communications we have answered this question in one form or another.

Think on this question deeply, and then act accordingly, taking no thought, and you will discover a spring of hidden power that will bring to pass miracles undreamed of by the purely human self.

June 13, 1978

Center thy conscious awareness this day on the Son, the great shining Son of God which is centered, or held in place within thee by thy conscious Being or the I AM which eternally affirms this Truth. This I AM, or affirmation of conscious life is the Point wherein the infinitude of God's life is focused.

All during this fresh new day that lies before thee, remind thyself constantly of this tremendous fact, that the fullness of God's Presence is centered within thine own self awareness from instant to instant even as the breath of life flows into thy body and out of thy body from instant to instant.

There can be no moment when this Truth is not operating, is not fully present whether thou art conscious of it or not. The purpose of thy life is to be conscious of it. Think deeply on this. There can be no instant when God's presence is not fully within reach of thy conscious being, as thy Self, thy immortal Selfhood. Therefore, cease thy fostering of this human creature, but see only thy God Self as the One reality of thy existence, not to be realized in some future heaven, but to be known here and now, in this place, at this time. Even so will thy God Self come forth and become thy self, closing the gap between the human and the divine.

January 21, 1979

We have said a great and glorious destiny awaits you and all those, who dedicate their lives to Truth, to God but you must do your part—to become entangled with the small, unknowing attributes of the ego, blocks the flow of Truth—you *know* this, so watch, we say, watch how the mechanism works—how the thoughts that the ego creates so often consumes the fires of Truth—so what do you have? Ashes, nothing but ashes, and what can be built with ashes?

You have been given much Truth from the Inner Sanctuary—Unless the Light from this center becomes sovereign in you life's patterns now, you will miss the Destiny we speak of.

Hearken to our worlds this day for nothing can be concealed from Him who is Truth, who is Christ, and who is watching and waiting.

Amen.

November 2, 1981

What does it mean to be the image and likeness of God? It is very simple to understand and the Truth within this phrase is self-evident. God has created man a living soul, even as a mirror, in which to reflect himself-

Mans responsibility is to keep the mirror clear and unstained that God's Image may shine forth in all its' splendor and loveliness, unobstructed by the debris and dist which accumulates from false self or world self.

(A vision)

From where I stood
In the strange wood
I saw It.

Gazing in wonder
As the waters rose and fell,

A Fountain of Light
Emblazoning
The wood.

This was no earthly
Familiar thing,
These living waters
Flowered forth
Into the dusk,
And fell again
More softly,
More silently

Than falling light,

I stood transfixed
In ecstasy,
Breaking the solitude
With a cry!

O Loveliness,

O God….
O Radiance….
Unutterable.

Even as I marveled
The veil was drawn again;
The rapturous waters
Uplifted before mine eyes
Flowed forth no longer

The twilit wood,
The pale flowers
All had vanished.

Only love stood there,
And he folded his arms
About me,
Calling my name
In dear familiarity
Over and over.

(In visions and dreams of the night we are instructed)
Job.

England

www.ingramcontent.com/pod-product-compliance
Lightning Source LLC
LaVergne TN
LVHW050631100826
845148LV00011B/1834

* 9 7 8 0 9 8 1 6 4 6 7 2 5 *